· WARD LOCK MASTER GARDENER ·

Plant Propagation

FRED DOWNHAM

WARD LOCK

First published in Great Britain in 1993
by Ward Lock Limited, Villiers House, 41/47 Strand,
London WC2N 5JE, England
A Cassell Imprint

British Library in Cataloguing data for this book is available upon application to The British Library

ISBN 0 7063 7140 2

Text filmset by Litho Link Ltd, Welshpool, Powys
Printed and bound in Singapore by Craft Print Pte Ltd

Previous page: It is very rewarding to propagate your own plants and there are many easy ways of doing it.

Contents

◀ **Saving your own seeds is a very economical way of creating a colourful garden.**

Preface

You can create an instant garden by buying in ready-grown plants, but it is very expensive and it isn't anywhere near as satisfying as growing your own. They can be raised from seed, cuttings, layering or by various other simple methods, most of which are covered in this book. If you haven't already got plants from which to propagate, you'll find that gardeners are usually generous people and will be only too pleased to give you seeds, cuttings, etc., but do ask first. I have covered the most important points on propagation, but in a book this size it is impossible to go into it in great detail; however I hope I have managed to offer enough tips and information to get you started. You will find line drawings to help you along the way and coloured photographs of some of the plants included. Once you see those tiny seedlings pushing through the compost or roots forming on your cuttings, I guarantee you will want to raise more and more. Your garden will gradually fill up with plants you have raised yourself, many of which will bring back fond memories of where they were originally acquired and the people who gave them to you.

If a particular plant is not in the index, you should find it in the alphabetical lists in Chapters 10–16, together with the easiest methods of propagation which are described in the earlier chapters.

May I wish you happy gardening and successful propagating.

F.D.

ACKNOWLEDGEMENTS

The publishers would like to thank the following for supplying photographs for this book: Pat Brindley: p. 17; Fred Downham: pp. 1, 12, 16, 20, 26, 29, 32, 40 (bottom), 49, 69, 72, 80, 88 (top left, bottom right), 92; Photos Horticultural Picture Library: pp. 4, 9, 21, 24, 28, 33, 45, 48, 61, 73, 77, 88 (top right, bottom left), 89; Harry Smith: pp. 37, 40 (top), 53, 56, 64 (left).

The line illustrations were drawn by David Woodroffe, except for the following: Vana Haggerty F.L.S.: pp. 66, 75, 78, 79, 82, 85, 91; Nils Solberg: pp. 57, 94.

· 1 · Essential Equipment

You don't have to have a lot of sophisticated equipment and tools to propagate plants successfully, although they do make life easier and they will guarantee you a higher success rate. You can manage with everyday items; plastic drinking cups and tubs will substitute for pots and seed trays. Lollipop sticks will make perfectly adequate labels and fingers were around a long time before dibbers.

If you haven't got a greenhouse, you can make use of your window sills, but remember that plants could become drawn and leggy because of inadequate light. Hardening off plants in a cold frame is quite easy; without one it's a case of putting them outside during the day and carrying them back indoors at night, especially if temperatures are likely to drop.

You don't need every piece of equipment covered in this chapter, just choose those relevant to the methods of propagation you wish to carry out.

TOOLS

Buying cheap tools is false economy; good, well-made ones should last a lifetime, but do make sure that they are right for you. Handles need to be the correct length and tools such as secateurs need to fit your hand comfortably. Try out different sizes before you buy.

Outdoor tools (Fig. 1, page 10)
You will need a larger selection of tools for working outdoors than you will for indoor use.

- *A spade* is necessary to do the initial digging and any other earth moving operations.
- *A border fork* will also be needed in order to break down the soil and remove any weeds, or for lifting plants to obtain root cuttings etc.
- *A garden rake* is essential for levelling seed beds and for producing a fine tilth prior to sowing.
- *A swan-necked hoe* will enable you to draw out flat-bottomed drills for sowing such as peas and beans.
- *A hand trowel* will be useful for such jobs as digging up small plants to divide them, or for making holes for large seeds and tubers.
- *A dibber* is useful for making holes. A broken spade or fork shaft with a pointed end is ideal for this and you'll find that the sharp end can also be used to draw out drills when sowing seeds.
- *Measuring equipment* In order to get your lines straight, you need a measuring stick which can be made from a broom handle marked off every 8 cm (3 in). You will also need a good strong garden line which won't break when pulled taut across the bed.

• *A watering can* with a coarse rose or a spray nozzle attached to a hosepipe will make watering outdoors easy.

• *Labels*, preferably 20 × 2.5 cm (8 × 1 in), are necessary at the end of each row to remind you exactly what you have sown or planted. Write on them with a waterproof marking pen or a soft-leaded pencil.

• *A good pair of secateurs* are necessary for taking and preparing hardwood cuttings, as well as a *knife* with a pointed blade and a flat, wedge-shaped handle which will come in useful when budding or grafting. Both these implements should be very sharp so that you make a good, clean cut.

Greenhouse tools

• *Containers* When working indoors, the most important pieces of equipment are pots of various sizes made from plastic or clay, and seed trays – standard, half size or quarter size – depending on requirements. Or you may prefer to use divided inserts for sowing or pricking out.

• *Composts* There are various types of compost and the one you use will depend on which job you are doing. Choose the appropriate one from the chart here.

• *Tampers* Once the containers have been filled, firm the compost with a tamper. You'll need various shapes and sizes to fit the containers. They can be specially made, but there are always household items with smooth bases, such as a box, a piece of wood or the bottom or lid of a jar, which will do the job adequately.

• *A hand sprayer* with a nozzle that will produce a fine spray for watering newly sown seeds will ensure that they don't get washed to one end of the container, and for damping the leaves of cuttings whilst they are rooting.

• *Additional equipment.* A small *dibber* is useful for pricking out and inserting cuttings, a *fine sieve* for dusting compost over small seeds and an *old dinner fork* to raise seedlings etc. out of the compost when moving them on.

Certain seeds, such as sweet peas, require a *seed dressing* and it's always better to plunge cuttings in a *fungicide* and dip the wounds in a powder or liquid *hormone rooting agent* before planting them.

· COMPOSTS AND THEIR USES ·

Name	*Use*
Soil based	
John Innes Seed	Seeds and cuttings
John Innes No.1	Pricking out, potting in small pots.
John Innes No.2	Potting in pots up to 13cm (5 in)
John Innes No.3	Large pots and containers
Multi-purpose Loam	General
Peat based	
All Purpose Seed and Potting	General
Multi-purpose	Seeds, cuttings, potting
Potting and Container	Pots and containers
Universal	General
Seed and Cutting	Seeds and cuttings
Ericaceous	General for acid-loving plants
Low peat	
Organic multi-purpose	General
Peat free	
Coir based	General
Multi-purpose Cocofibre	Seeds and potting
Coco compost	General
Peat Free Universal	General
Sterile mediums	
Perlite and Vermiculite	Add to compost for improved drainage and moisture retention

OTHER EQUIPMENT

Frames and cloches

Cold frames can be used to propagate a wide number of plants; however if you have a greenhouse, a cold frame is almost essential. One of their main uses is as a halfway stop for plants between the greenhouse and the garden, where they are hardened off before finally going outside. They are also used for raising seedlings that don't require high temperatures to germinate, such as brassicas, alpines etc. and early salad crops, and for rooting cuttings.

They can be all glass, have solid sides with glass or plastic tops – but these must be removable or adjustable to close, partly open or be fully open, depending on the weather.

You can use cloches in a similar way, but they have to be removed completely to carry out any work such as sowing, watering, weeding etc.

Plastic tunnels

A plastic tunnel is just like a large cloche, but high enough to walk into. It comprises a stout metal frame covered with a heavy-gauge polythene, very similar to a greenhouse, but they are colder in winter and warm up very quickly in the summer. However, it is possible to work inside them, offering protection to you as well as the plants. The initial cost is considerably lower than a greenhouse, but it is as well to bear in mind that the cover will need renewing about every three years and if you heat them, the running costs are higher.

PROPAGATORS

To germinate seeds and root most cuttings successfully, you really need a propagator and there are plenty to choose from. They include cold ones which consist of just a tray and a plastic top, heated ones which raise the temperature by several degrees, or the more expensive ones with adjustable thermostats which can be set to any temperature required. Most of these have vents that can be opened when necessary. If there is no power supply to the greenhouse, propagators are available heated by paraffin. These are quite economical, but you must make sure that they don't run out of fuel, and the temperature is not as easy to control.

Pots, seed trays and various containers needed for propagation.

· HANDY TIP ·

Tools will last longer and will be easier to work with if they are cleaned after being used before putting them away. Wash seed boxes, pots etc. immediately after emptying them so that they are ready for use whenever you require them. Don't ever fill dirty containers with clean compost.

It is possible to make your own propagator if there isn't one available to meet your requirements. You will need a deep-sided box with a polythene top and soil-warming cables buried in sand at the bottom. The cables are available in a choice of lengths to suit the size of area to be heated; they are either mains operated using a transformer and thermostat, or they can be low voltage to plug straight into the mains.

• *Mist units* If you intend to raise large numbers of cuttings, you may consider a mist unit. It comprises a box with soil-warming cables as above and an ingenious device called an electronic leaf fitted to a mains water supply. The misting unit is controlled by a censor which activates a solenoid valve. When the leaves of the cuttings dry, the misting spray is switched on and when they are moist enough the water is switched off. The leaves of the cuttings never dry out, they stay turgid at all times and roots are formed far quicker with very few losses. So, as well as a water supply, it also needs electricity.

Note: Any electricity supply should be fitted with an isolator and correctly installed by a qualified electrician to ensure safety at all times.

Fig. 1 Useful tools for propagating both out of doors and indoors.

KEY

1. Garden fork
2. Garden rake
3. Spade
4. Swan-necked hoe
5. Measuring stick
6. Hose
7. Hand trowel
8. Hand fork
9. Watering can
10. Garden line
11. Labels
12. Marker pen
13. Secateurs
14. Knife
15. Dibber
16. Pots
17. Seed tray
18. Divided tray

Greenhouses

Don't rush out and buy the first greenhouse you see. It's an expensive item so give it quite a lot of thought beforehand. The cost will almost certainly play a large part in your final decision, but greenhouses are like garages, they are never big enough, so always buy the largest you can afford that will fit into the allotted space. A standard 2.4 × 1.8 m (8 × 6 ft) aluminium alloy-framed greenhouse is normally the cheapest, but if possible you would be better buying a larger one, even though it will cost more. The disadvantage of these is that they lose heat very quickly when it's cold outside and temperatures rise rapidly when the sun shines. Wooden-framed greenhouses look more decorative, retain heat for a longer period and stay just that little bit cooler if we get a warm period, but they do need regular maintenance and they are more expensive. Most of them are made from red cedar and so need treating with a water-repellent wood preservative every three or four years and other woods will need painting at regular intervals. If you can afford the top of the range, there are aluminium alloy structures with a special paint finish which makes them even more durable and attractive.

Of course, the ultimate greenhouse is a wooden one built to your specifications and with double glazing.

- *Good ventilation* is essential and it's always better to add more vents to those provided with the basic greenhouse. Ideally, there should be several in the roof and sides and one in the end opposite the door, and they should all open automatically (Fig. 2).

- *Staging* (Fig. 3) will be needed for working on and for positioning your young plants so that they are near the glass and don't become drawn and leggy. When full, this will carry a lot of weight

Fig. 2 Install as many automatically opening ventilators as possible to achieve a good circulation of air. They open when the temperature inside reaches a certain level and are ideal for the unattended greenhouse.

Fig. 3 To create the correct conditions, staging should be slatted in winter and covered with capillary matting in the summer.

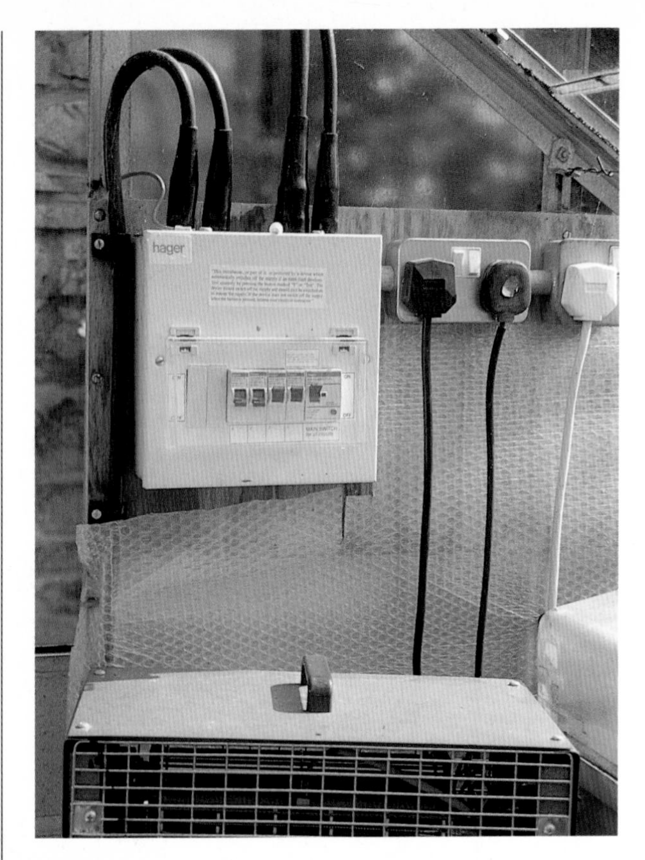

Any electricity supply should be fitted by a qualified electrician.

and so it needs to be substantial. If you are going to grow crops such as tomatoes at ground level at any time, at least one side of the staging should be easy to dismantle and store away.

• *Glazing* can be either glass or a glass substitute, such as plastic. Glass is still the best to use, but it can be dangerous where young children are concerned. Plastic or PVC deteriorates quite quickly and needs replacing every few years or you will lose valuable light. Twin-sided polycarbonate is quite durable, conserves heat like double glazing, but every five or six years it will need dismantling and the channels washed out to remove any dirt.

Greenhouses should always be positioned in full light and as near to the house as possible so that you have easy and cheap access to mains electricity and water.

Heating

If you can provide heat in your greenhouse you will be able to propagate a wide range of plants.

• *Paraffin heaters* may be the easiest to install, but they do need regular attention – filling and cleaning.

• *Solid fuel systems* are still available, but they can be costly and time consuming to run and you need storage space for the fuel.

• *Gas* is another alternative which is quite efficient. You need a back-up cylinder for bottled gas and, if you are using the mains, you need an electricity supply as well.

• *Electricity* is without a doubt the cleanest of all and if you use a thermostatically controlled heater, it works out the cheapest to run as it only uses power when necessary. If it is a fan heater, it will also circulate the air. If the heating elements and the fan are controlled separately, the fan can be used in summer to keep the air moving, so lowering the temperature which will help to prevent diseases.

You can conserve heat by lining the greenhouse with bubble polythene, this will save fuel during the colder months.

A greenhouse can get very hot during the summer and plants can be scorched by the sun. Prevent this from happening by applying one of the special paints to the glass or by using a greenhouse shading material which can be taken down easily if the weather changes.

▶ Propagation is easier in a well-equipped greenhouse.

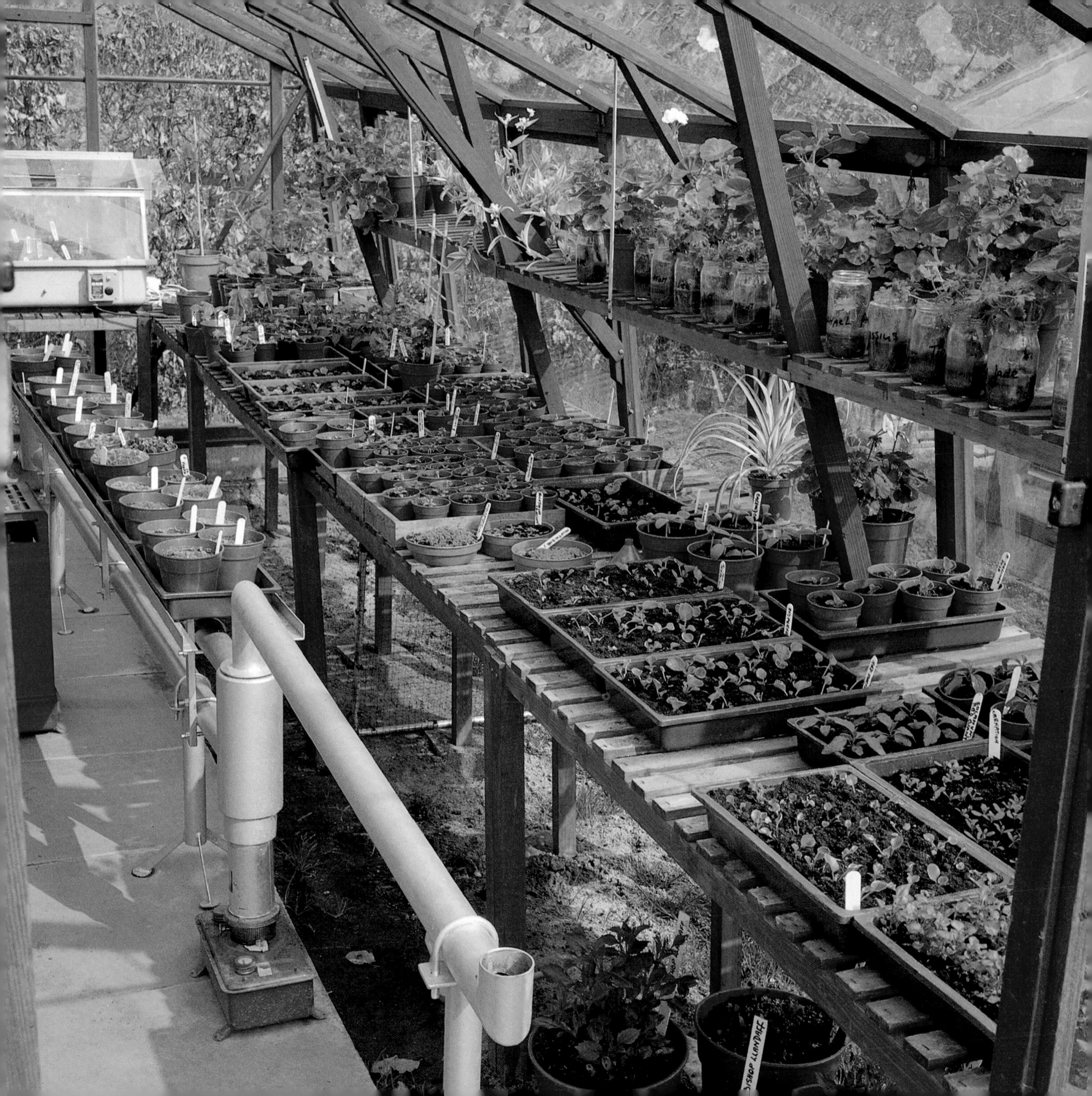

· 2 ·
All About Seed

Raising plants from seed is one of the most interesting aspects of gardening. We sow them, wait for them to come through, nurture them through their early days and they reward us with beautiful flowers or tasty produce. Not only will you get a terrific sense of satisfaction, but it is also one way of filling your garden with plants at a very reasonable cost.

HARVESTING SEED FROM THE GARDEN

Seeds should only be gathered when they are perfectly ripe and in prime condition. Taken too early, they may not be viable, but if you leave them too late they may be shed naturally and lost. Collect them on a fine day when the seed heads are nice and dry. If you pick them when it is damp, they are likely to go mouldy in store.

Flowers

• *Poppies* These shed their seeds very quickly. You have only to touch the seed pod when ripe and it will burst open, dispersing its contents. It is safer to enclose the head in a paper or muslin bag. Hang it up in a warm, dry place and the seeds will drop into it.

• *Legumes* Sweet peas, lupins etc. produce green pods which turn brown as they become ready for collecting. Flick the pod with your finger and if the seeds rattle, they are ready. If not, check again in another couple of days. Cut them, place them in a paper bag and hang them in a warm, dry place. They will split open and curl when they are perfectly dry.

• *Violas and hellebores* These plants have seed capsules which stay green when the seed is ripe. When you think that they look full it is as well to open one carefully and check. If the seed is dark brown it is ripe and can be harvested. If it's green it is immature and needs to be left a while longer.

• *Anemones* Some seeds stay green when ripe and never turn brown. Anemones are a good example of this. Keep your eye on them. If you touch one of the seed pods and it bursts, this is a sure indication that the rest are ready for taking.

Vegetables and fruit

The seed should not be gathered until vegetables and fruit are fully ripe. Don't allow the tomatoes to fall, otherwise the seed will be bruised. The safest way is to support them by enclosing them in a fine net.

Trees

Collecting seed from trees can be difficult as most of them are carried on the ends of thin branches near the top of the tree. If you are unable to reach them from a ladder, it is far safer to let them fall naturally. Luckily, most seed is hard and, as long as it is gathered quickly, it will not be harmed.

If you grow a wide range of plants it will take a while to know when some of them are ready. There may be times when you lose some of them, but you will eventually get it right.

DRYING AND STORING

Once the seeds have been harvested they should be completely dried. Spread them out on newspaper in a light, airy place – a greenhouse bench or on a window sill indoors or hang them up in paper bags. Some will take longer than others to become fully dry. Renew the newspaper or bags if they feel damp.

Cleaning the seed

When perfectly dry, tip them onto clean, dry paper and burst any seed capsules that are still whole. Remove any debris and then pass what is left through a sieve (Fig. 4).

Even then there will still be a certain amount of dried plant material amongst the seeds and this should be removed. If you tip the seeds slowly from one paper to another, blowing as you do it, you should clear most of it. If you find any insects, destroy them before storing or they may damage some of the seeds.

Storing

If seeds are stored too hot and dry or damp, they will be damaged. One of the best ways is to place them in sealed paper envelopes, one for each variety, and name them. Place the packets in a screw top jar with a sachet of silica gel to absorb excess moisture and store them in the salad drawer of the refrigerator. If ripe and dried correctly, most seed should stay viable in store for a few years.

Seeds collected from F1 varieties will not come true. They will be varied and, unless you don't mind what you raise, it's better not to waste your time sowing them.

QUALITY CONTROL

When collecting seeds you must be very selective. It is important only to take them from plants that are true to type, vigorous and healthy, which means checking the parents at regular intervals throughout the season. Mark the best ones and if any of these show signs of deterioration, don't use them.

Look for the best coloured flowers and good, clean foliage. If they are vegetables, use those which crop well, have the best flavour and are a good texture.

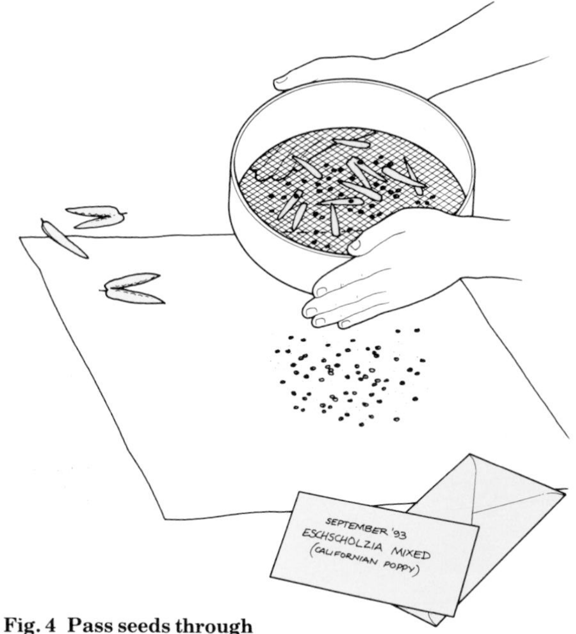

Fig. 4 Pass seeds through a sieve to remove any debris.

Once you have decided which plants you will be using for seed, mark them early in the season so that they will ripen in the better weather. If you leave it too late the seed may not have time to mature fully and, even if it does, it may not ripen properly.

BUYING SEED

If you are buying your seeds from a garden shop or by mail order, don't get carried away. The coloured pictures in catalogues and on packets can be very tempting and you may find yourself ordering far too many.

When you first start growing from seed it will be a case of trial and error. Gradually you will discover your favourites, but always be prepared to try one or two new ones. Remember to order early, otherwise you will find that some of the varieties are sold out.

SEED TYPES

Prime seeds

Some of the more difficult seeds to germinate, such as begonias and verbena, are now offered as prime seeds. These are partially germinated, then suspended before they are packeted. When we sow them they come through quicker at lower temperatures.

Pelleted seed

If you don't want to go to the trouble of pricking out or thinning, use pelleted seed (Fig. 5). These are enclosed in a special coating, about as big as a small pea, but they do need treating differently from ordinary seed. Read the instructions and follow them carefully.

F1 hybrids

F1 hybrids are the first generation after crossing two selected parents. They are bred for uniformity, height, etc. They are always more expensive, because producing them is very labour intensive.

◄ A technician checks seeds for quality and germination under controlled conditions.

► As with all plants, the seeds of *Clematis orientalis* must be ripe before they are gathered.

Fig. 5 Sowing large and small seeds in containers.

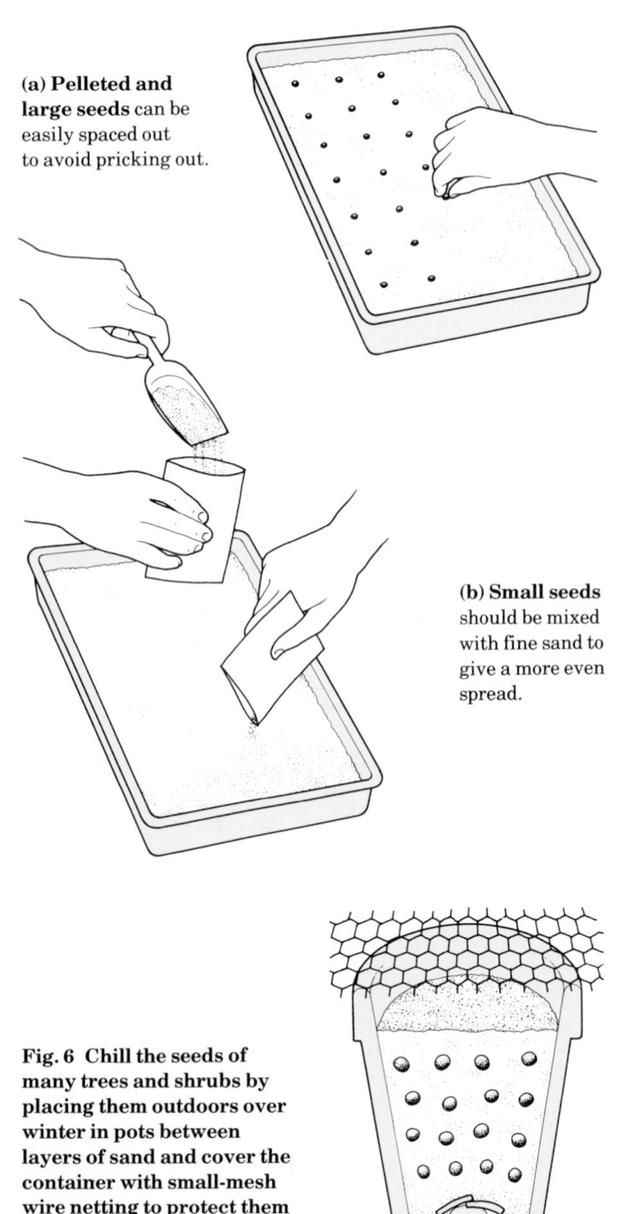

(a) Pelleted and large seeds can be easily spaced out to avoid pricking out.

(b) Small seeds should be mixed with fine sand to give a more even spread.

Fig. 6 Chill the seeds of many trees and shrubs by placing them outdoors over winter in pots between layers of sand and cover the container with small-mesh wire netting to protect them from vermin, etc.

F2 hybrids

These are the result of allowing F1 varieties to pollinate freely, isolated from other plants that may interfere with pollination. They are not as expensive as F1 varieties.

Germination control

Seedsmen are often blamed for poor germination, but more often than not it's our fault. The seeds are tested thoroughly and, as long as we give them the right conditions, we will get good results. They will take perhaps 50 seeds at random from a batch, place them in petri dishes in a growing chamber, all under sterile conditions and at exactly the correct temperature, and if the germination level is not up to standard they are rejected.

REQUIREMENTS FOR GERMINATION

Seeds need different conditions to germinate. Some need high temperatures whilst others like to be cool and quite a number need cold treatment to break their dormancy (Fig. 6).

- *Light* Certain ones germinate best in light, so sow these on the surface of the compost. Others prefer to be placed in the dark.

- *Hard coated seeds*, such as sweet peas, germinate better if they have been soaked to soften the outer skin. Very dark seeds may have to be chipped which entails breaking the skin on the opposite side to the eye without damaging the delicate inner part, but allowing moisture to penetrate.

- *Inhibitors* Some seeds such as cyclamen have a coating, which, if not removed, prevents them from germinating. This must be washed off in tepid water before sowing.

· 3 ·

Seed Sowing Outdoors

Most vegetables and hardy annuals can be grown by sowing the seed directly outdoors. Brassicas are sown in outdoor seed beds or in the shelter of a cold frame and transplanted into their cropping positions later, as are biennials and a lot of perennials. Alpines, trees and shrubs do not require high temperatures to germinate. These can be sown in pots, seed pans or boxes and placed outdoors.

SOIL PREPARATION AND SOWING

When sowing directly into the ground it is important that the soil is well prepared. Dig a trench in the autumn so that the soil can be left all through the winter months to be broken down by frost or rain. This way, in spring it will be much easier to work and get into the right condition for sowing. On no condition work on soil that is wet and sticky, particularly if it is clayey. Far better to wait until it is reasonably dry.

Improving the soil

Whilst turning the soil over, remove the roots of perennial weeds and if the soil is heavy add quite large amounts of grit to improve the drainage. On light soils it is beneficial to add plenty of well-rotted farmyard manure or garden compost to retain moisture.

Soil testing

Check whether your soil is acid or alkaline by carrying out a pH test. pH 7 is neutral; add lime to raise the level or flowers of sulphur to lower it. Most plants grow well at a pH of 6.5.

Warming the soil

Once cultivated, cover the ground with sheets of polythene or cloches to warm it up and keep it dry so that you can sow earlier, thus cropping whilst vegetables are in short supply in the shops.

Don't be in too big a hurry to make a start on the rest of the garden, wait until the weather improves. Seeds sown in cold, wet soil may rot and those sown later soon catch up.

Feeding the soil

In spring, when the soil is dry and reasonably warm, fork over the ground, breaking down any clods in the process and level it out as you go. If you are not able to dig until spring, leave it to settle for a few weeks before sowing. Then add a general fertilizer which contains equal amounts of nitrogen, phosphates and potash at 57–85 g (2–3 oz) per square yard.

Rake the fertilizer into the top couple of inches with the back of a fork and trample the soil down with your feet. Then rake it to create a fine tilth and remove any large stones.

◀ Warm the soil in late winter by covering it with cloches or polythene to enable you to sow earlier.

▶ Sow French beans 15 cm (6 in) apart in a single row.

Sowing

• *Small seeds* are sown in shallow drills 13 mm (½ in) deep and each row should be 30–38 cm (12–15 in) apart. Use a measuring stick and a taut line to achieve this (Fig. 7). Make them straight and evenly spaced, then make the drill with either the corner of a swan-necked hoe or pointed length of broom handle.

It doesn't matter how careful you are when sowing continuous rows of seeds, some thinning will have to be done later.

Alternatively, you can space sow, dropping three or four seeds at each station. This way you will not use as many and there should not be as much thinning to do.

• *Large seeds* such as garden peas and broad beans are sown in a flat-bottomed drill 5 cm (2 in) deep and 20 cm (8 in) wide. These will hold three staggered rows of peas spaced approximately 10 cm (4 in) apart, or just scatter them along the length of the row so that they are evenly spaced.

Sow tall-growing varieties of broad beans in a double row along either side of the wide drill, spacing them 20 cm (8 in) apart. Sow the dwarf varieties in a single row, as they make bushier plants. These are ideal for growing under cloches.

Dwarf French beans also go in a single row, spacing the seeds 15 cm (6 in) apart. If you have more than one row, these should have 50 cm (20 in) between them.

Label each row so that you know exactly what you have sown.

If the soil is very dry, soak the bottom of the drill before sowing and then cover them with dry soil to seal in the moisture.

Once the seeds are in and covered, tamp down the soil with the back of a rake.

Sowing in a seed bed

Sow brassicas, biennials or perennials in a seed bed in full light. The rows can be much closer together, 20 cm (8 in) apart, as they will be transplanted later.

Sowing directly into ground

Hardy annuals are sown directly into the beds where they are to flower. Prepare the ground as you would for a seed bed, but unless it is very impoverished, don't add fertilizer as they do not like a rich soil.

Once dug, firmed and raked, mark out the bed with a pointed stick into irregular blocks of varying shapes and sizes, so that it finishes up like a patchwork quilt, taking into account height, form and colour.

Draw 13 mm (½ in) deep drills, 10–15 cm (4–6 in) apart across each one, changing direction slightly in each patch. Then sow the seeds sparingly, cover them lightly, firm down the soil and water if necessary.

Alternatively, scatter the seed broadcast in each section, but it can then be difficult to tell the plants from the weeds. Whichever way you choose to sow, they will require thinning later.

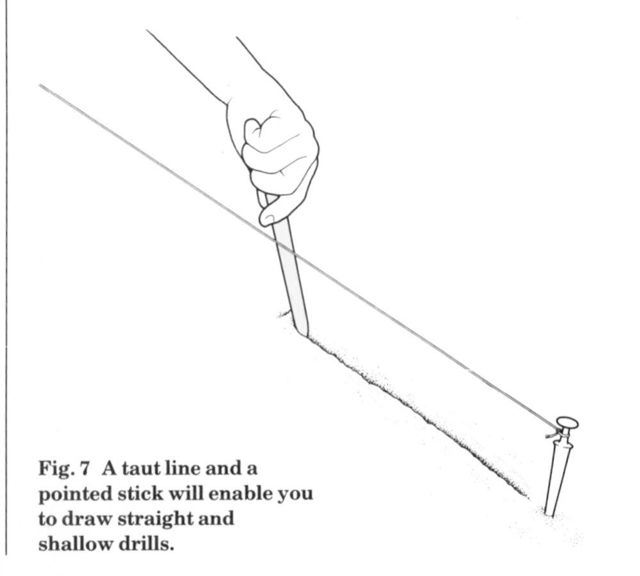

Fig. 7 A taut line and a pointed stick will enable you to draw straight and shallow drills.

· HANDY TIP ·

To avoid overcrowding when sowing small seeds into drills, tip a few into the palm of your hand and spread them, using the finger and thumb of your other hand. Or drop a few at each station to make thinning easier.

Sowing a lawn

Making a lawn from seed is far cheaper than laying turves. It takes longer to establish, but you will have a far greater choice of types of grass, depending on what the lawn is to be used for.

Preparing the area is just like creating a large seed bed, but do give it plenty of time to settle after the initial digging or you could end up with bumps and hollows.

The best way to get an even spread of seed is to mark out the area into metres or yard squares using garden lines and canes for guidance. Then scatter approximately 42 g (1½ oz) of the seed over each measured square without leaving any gaps. Then rake the seed in lightly and compress it with a roller (the one on the mower will do). Water it and if cats or birds are a nuisance, cover it with strong garden netting.

Sowing in pots

• *Alpines* Most alpines can be raised quite easily in pots or pans filled with well-drained compost, (John Innes seed compost with 25 per cent extra fine grit added is ideal). Level it, press it down and scatter the seeds thinly. Cover them with a thin layer of grit, water them and place them outdoors.

If it freezes or they are covered with snow, this is all to the good. When the weather warms up in spring the seed will germinate more freely if it has been chilled previously.

• *Hardy trees and shrubs* are sown in exactly the same way as alpines, but it does help if the seed is subjected to a cold, damp period beforehand. This is known as stratification.

Place the seeds between layers of sand in a vermin-proof container with drainage holes. Bury it outdoors – the colder the better – and sow them in the normal way in spring.

Fluid sowing

Fluid sowing is often recommended, particularly in soils which are slow to warm up in spring or for varieties that take quite a while to germinate and need a long growing season, such as parsnips. The seed is pre-germinated indoors (this process is known as chitting), by placing them in damp kitchen paper in a sealed plastic container in a warm place at around 16°C (60°F). Check them every day and as soon as you see any sign of growth, watch them carefully.

When the roots and shoots are 6 mm (¼ in) long, they should be mixed in an alginate gel, or you could use wallpaper paste at twice the normal dilution, but it must be one that does not contain a fungicide.

Stir them very carefully to disperse the seed evenly throughout the gel. Then place them in a strong polythene bag with a corner cut off and sow them by squeezing the bag so that the gel and seeds drop through the hole. You can either sow one continuous row in the drill or place a drop of gel every so often along the row, making sure that each one contains a few seeds.

Cover them in the normal way, tamp them down and, if it is a very hot day, water the drills overhead. Give them a thorough soaking or the paste may set, preventing the seeds from pushing through.

Chitted seed

It is possible to sow the chitted seed directly into the soil without using any gel, but conditions must be ideal and it should be done with great

· STORING VEGETABLE SEED ·

The following chart gives the life expectancy of stored vegetable seed under normal conditions.

Vegetable	Time	Vegetable	Time
Artichoke globe	2 years	Kale	3 years
Asparagus	2 years	Kohl Rabi	2 years
Aubergine	5 years	Leek	2 years
Bean		Lettuce	2 years
• broad	2 years	Marrow	4 years
• dwarf French	2 years	Melon	2 years
• runner	2 years	Onion	1 year
• climbing French	2 years	Pak choi	2 years
Beetroot	2 years	Parsnip	1 year
Broccoli	3 years	Pea	2 years
Brussels sprout	3 years	Pepper	4 years
Cabbage	3 years	Pumpkin	3 years
Carrot	4 years	Radish	4 years
Cauliflower	2 years	Salsify	2 years
Celeriac	4 years	Scorzonera	2 years
Celery	4 years	Spinach	3 years
Chicory	4 years	Spinach beet	2 years
Courgette	4 years	Swede	2 years
Cucumber	5 years	Sweetcorn	2 years
Endive	4 years	Tomato	4 years
Florence Fennel	2 years	Turnip	2 years

◀ **Fluid sowing: Pre-germinated seed can be sown mixed with a gel, using a plastic bag with the corner cut off.**

▶ **A well-tended vegetable plot can look as attractive as a flower border.**

care as you could easily damage or break the delicate shoots. The soil must be moist and never be allowed to dry out.

If you have sprouted the seed, but you are unable to sow them immediately, you can hold them back for a few days by leaving them sealed in the container in the salad drawer of the refrigerator.

Thinning

Every seed we sow needs room to grow once it has germinated. No matter how sparingly we drop them into the drills, they have to be either transplanted or thinned out by removing some of the seedlings, leaving the remainder to develop fully.

This also applies to those sown a few per station. Do this as soon as the seedlings are large enough to handle. Pull out the weakest, leaving the strongest as long as they are at the right spacings. Try not to disturb the ones that are going to be left in, hold the soil firmly round the roots whilst you remove the rest with your other hand (Fig. 8).

If there is a gap in the row where some have failed to germinate, lift one of the unwanted seedlings carefully and replant it to fill the space.

This job is best done when the ground is moist, but if you have to thin them during a dry period, press the soil back around the roots and give them a good watering.

Spacings do vary and the seed packet usually gives you the correct one for each variety.

Transplanting

If you have sown in a seed bed, transplant the seedlings of biennials and perennials into a nursery bed once they reach a height of 10–15 cm (4–6 in). This should be prepared a few days in advance, by digging it over and forking in a general fertilizer at 57 g (2 oz) per square yard. Then firm to consolidate the soil, so that the seedlings will be transplanted securely.

If the seedlings are transferred to the nursery bed when the ground is moist, they will re-establish themselves quickly and will hardly know they have been moved. Lift them carefully with a fork and transplant them, making the holes with a trowel. They won't need as much room as they will when they are finally planted, just give them 20 cm (8 in) between the plants and 30 cm (12 in) between the rows. They go into their final positions later.

Brassicas, leeks, lettuces, etc. go straight from the nursery bed into their cropping positions as soon as they are large enough to handle.

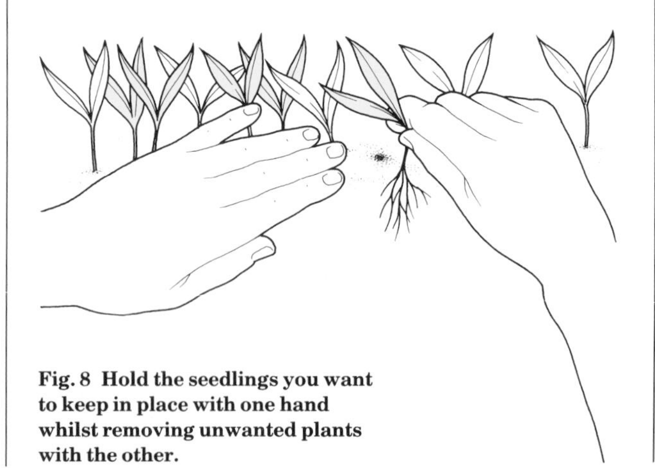

Fig. 8 Hold the seedlings you want to keep in place with one hand whilst removing unwanted plants with the other.

· HANDY TIP ·

In dry weather water the seed bed a few hours before transplanting the seedlings, then puddle the plants in when you transfer them. Make the hole, fill it with water, allow it to soak in, plant and cover up the roots with dry soil to prevent the sun from drawing out the moisture.

Controlling weeds

The best way to control weeds is to hoe between the rows and the plants weekly, weather permitting, even if there are none to be seen. This is best done on a sunny day so that the germinating weed seedlings will be killed, but even if it is dull, it will check them and stop them from growing strongly.

Any growing near to the plants must be pulled out by hand later, as soon as they are large enough to get hold of.

Once the plants are growing strongly and the foliage meets and covers the ground, there will be very few weeds to clear. However, there are always one or two that escape so keep your eyes open and pull them out before they seed, otherwise there will be many more the following year. Bear in mind the old saying 'One year's seeding means seven year's weeding', it's very true.

· 4 ·

Seed Sowing Under Glass

The greatest advantage of sowing seeds under cover is that you are able to create the correct conditions for germination. You provide the right compost and temperatures that each variety needs, you can water them exactly when they need it, either from above or below, and you will be able to choose from far more varieties.

Young seedlings will be protected from the weather and therefore you will have a far greater chance of raising them successfully.

The main sowings are carried out from winter through to mid-spring, depending on whether they are slow growing such as geraniums (zonal pelargoniums) and lobelia or, for instance, alyssum and asters which do not take as long from sowing to flowering. It is all a matter of timing so that your young bedding plants are at just the right stage of growth for planting out at the end of spring or the first two weeks of summer when the soil is starting to warm up and there is very little chance of frost or chilling winds. Conditions vary by as much as four weeks, depending on where you live. Once you know when it is safe to plant out, you will be able to calculate your sowing dates from the information on the seed packets and in the catalogues.

Containers

The size of container you use depends on how many seedlings of each variety you wish to raise.

- *Standard seed trays* will hold 50 large seeds, but hundreds of small ones. If you don't want this many, you can use a half tray.
- *Pots* can be used for smaller numbers. You can get 30–40 seedlings in a 8 cm (3 in) one or twice that amount in a 13 cm (5 in) pot. Because seedlings are not deep rooted you can save on compost if you use the shallow half pots, and if you use any of these instead of seed trays you will be able to germinate more varieties in a propagator at one time.

Composts

When sowing seeds it is important that you only use specially prepared sterile composts. The main ingredient can be soil – as in John Innes seed compost – peat, coir or one of the many peat free alternatives. Do not use garden soil unless you sterilize it yourself, as it could contain pests and diseases which would ruin your seedlings.

Sowing (Fig. 9, page 30)

To get good germination, seeds must be sown at an even depth. Fill the container up to the rim, press it down slightly with your fingers, paying particular attention to any corners and smooth out any bumps and hollows. When it is perfectly level, press it down again with a tamper and then soak the compost by standing the pot or box in 2.5 cm (1 in) of water until the whole surface is damp.

◀ You will get better germination from some seeds if they are sown in a heated propagator.

▶ Don't forget to label your seeds once they have been sown.

Seeds can be sown directly onto the moist compost, but to get better results and prevent damping off, put 3 mm (1/8 in) layer of seed grade vermiculite on top of the compost, firm it and immediately sow the seeds.

The size of seeds varies considerably. Large ones such as sweet peas are easy to handle and can be spaced out separately, but the very fine seed of begonias, for instance, are like dust. These can be mixed evenly with a small quantity of fine, dry silver sand before sowing or, with practice, you can sow them sparingly off a piece of white paper folded down the middle (see again Fig. 5, page 18).

To save wasting seedlings when pricking out, sow seeds in rows 2.5 cm (1 in) apart. This is particularly helpful with lobelia as these are pricked out in small clumps rather than individually.

Once sown, press the seeds lightly into the compost or vermiculite, using the tamper, but make sure that it is clean and dry or it may pick up the seeds. It is always a good idea to get into the habit of wiping it with a piece of clean cloth each time you use it.

Most seed packets will tell you whether or not the seeds you are sowing need a covering of compost or whether they should be left exposed on

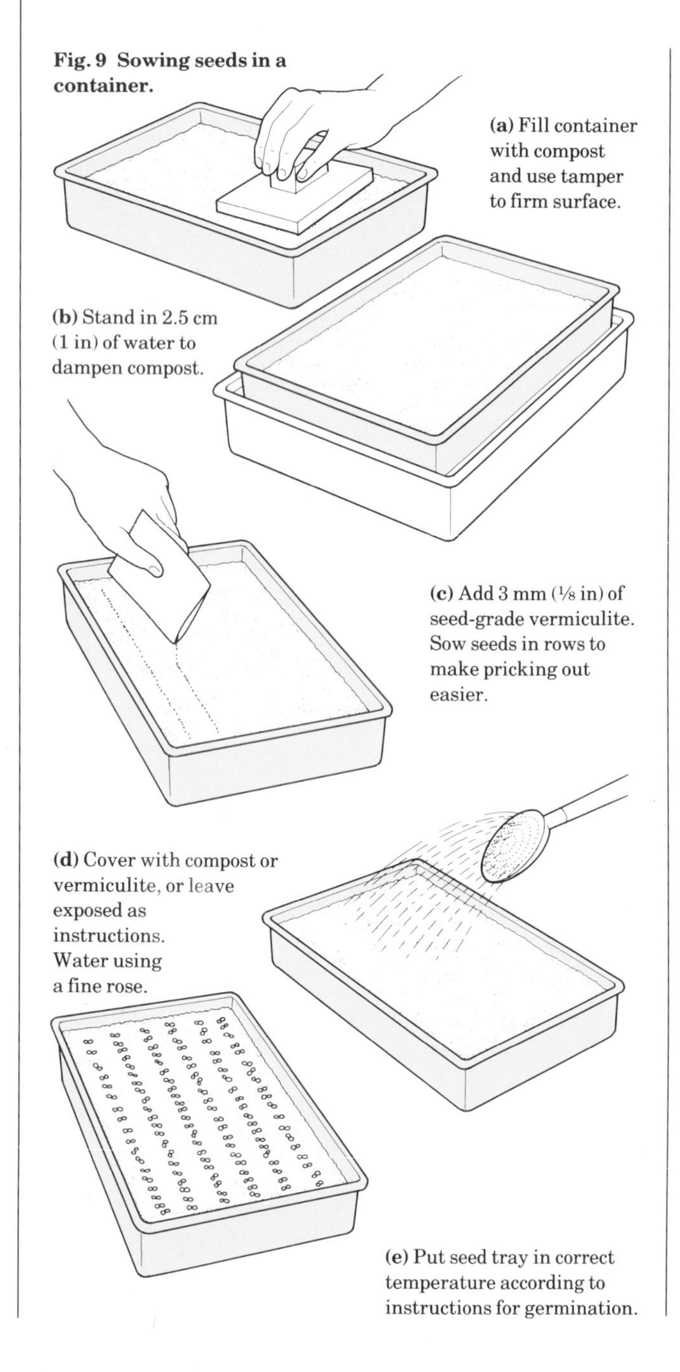

Fig. 9 Sowing seeds in a container.

the surface. As a rough guide, fine seeds stay uncovered and larger ones will need a covering of compost as deep as the size of seed e.g. sweet pea seeds are 6 mm (1/4 in) deep so they will need a 6 mm (1/4 in) covering of compost or vermiculite if you have used it. Whichever you use, press it down lightly to make sure that the seeds come into contact with it.

Water them using a watering can with a fine rose or, better still, a hand pressure spray which produces a fine mist. Give them a good soaking so that they don't dry out too quickly. Surface sown seeds such as busy lizzies (impatiens) and begonias should never be allowed to dry out. So once they have been sown, cover the container with cling-film or clear plastic to retain moisture (Fig. 10).

Put them in a temperature suitable for germination to take place (this depends on what you are sowing, so check the packet or seed catalogue). This is easy if you have a heated propagator with an adjustable thermostat, but it is possible to get good results by using a cold propagator placed in an airing cupboard, on a window sill in a warm room or on a shelf above a radiator. If it means using a dark cupboard, they must be transferred to a light position at the first sign of growth. If you leave them for just an hour or two once they have come through, they will elongate, become weak and straggly and won't make good plants.

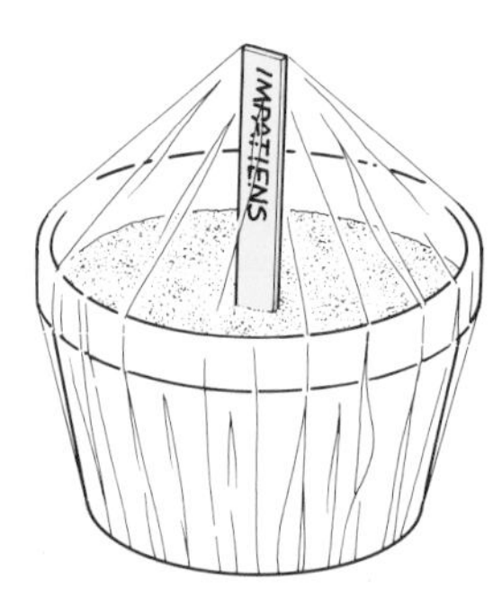

Fig. 10 Surface-sown seeds should never be allowed to dry out. Cover the container with clingfilm to retain moisture and stick the label in the centre of the container to prevent the clingfilm from sagging onto the seeds.

They should not be allowed to dry out, but avoid watering from above in the early stages as this may wash the tiny seedlings down onto the compost and they might never recover. Take them out of the propagator and stand the container in 2.5 cm (1 in) of tepid water so that the moisture is taken up from below. Let them drain and then return them to the warmth.

Temperature

The correct temperature is vital for good germination. Many house plants need a high one, whilst certain seeds such as lettuce are reluctant to germinate unless the temperature is kept below 16°C (60°F). In summer these are better sown in a cold frame rather than a greenhouse.

In cold districts hardy annuals can be sown in the cold frame or cold greenhouse in divided trays. Drop three or four seeds in each section and when they have grown to 2.5 cm (1 in) high, thin them down to one. This gives them an earlier start and prevents root disturbance when they are planted out. Some vegetables need to be started off under cover, especially in areas where the summers are short.

- *Brassicas, sweetcorn, marrows, outdoor tomatoes, etc.* can be sown in pots or divided trays in the shelter of a greenhouse or frame. The extra weeks of growth at the beginning of the season will ensure that crops are harvested before temperatures drop in the autumn.

- *Onions* need a long growing season and benefit from a late winter sowing under glass. One way to get a large crop of medium-sized bulbs is to multi-sow. Place six or seven seeds in each 9 cm (3½ in) pot, grow them on, harden them off and plant them out in early spring, still in a clump. This will more than double the weight gathered from a row than any planted singly.

- *Brassicas* Cold frames are also suitable for raising seedlings of cabbages, cauliflowers etc. and for starting off biennials such as wallflowers and forget-me-nots. Sow them straight into the soil of the frame, or use containers, or sow them and cover them with cloches.

Whatever you are sowing, resist the temptation to put too many seeds in for your needs. If you sow twelve lettuce seeds, they should produce at least ten lettuces which will all be ready at once. It is better to sow a few at regular intervals.

Hardening off

Once seedlings have germinated they should be acclimatized gradually to lower temperatures. Transfer those raised in a heated propagator to a cold one for a few days, then to the greenhouse bench. If they were started off in the greenhouse or on a window sill, take the tops of the propagators off during the day and replace them at night, leaving them off altogether after a week or so.

To prevent them from becoming drawn, they must be kept in good light at all times, but out of direct sun.

· HARDY ANNUALS ·

Hardy annuals that can be sown in autumn; outdoors in mild areas, under cold glass in exposed districts.

Adonis	Echium	Linum
Agrostemma	Euphorbia	Malope
Atriplex	Gilia	Mignonette
Bupleurum	Godetia	Nemophila
Calendula	Gypsophila	Nigella
Candytuft	Helipterum	Phacelia
Chrysanthemum	Larkspur	Poppy
Clarkia	Lavatera	Saponaria
Clary	Limnanthes	Scabious
Cornflower	Linanthus	Sweet pea
Crepis	Linaria	Viscaria

◄ **When pricking out into boxes, handle the seedlings by their leaves and start in the top corner.**

► **Sow your seeds in small pots and you will be able to get more varieties in a propagator at any one time.**

Pricking out

When seedlings have produced their first true leaves, prick them out. Lift them out of the compost carefully without breaking their roots (an old dinner fork is ideal for this job). Transfer them to a seed box or divided tray filled with a suitable potting compost. This will give them enough room to develop into sturdy plants. Hold them by a leaf, not the stems which can easily be damaged. Fill the container, firm the compost and, using a dibber, make a hole large enough to hold the roots comfortably. Put the seedlings in slightly deeper than it was previously, but don't bury the seed leaves. Push the compost back round the stem, pressing it down so that it is firmly planted.

If you are right-handed, start in the left hand corner furthest away from you, working across the long side of the tray and if you are left-handed, start at the opposite side. This means that you are working away from the seedlings already pricked out and so are far less likely to damage them.

If the variety is all one colour, choose the strongest seedlings, but if it is mixed, select ones of different heights and with leaves of varying shades of green so that you will end up with a good mixture.

Potting up

Some seedlings are potted up rather than pricked out. These include pot plants, tomatoes and geraniums (zonal pelargoniums) which need to grow into larger plants before they are planted out or potted on (moved into a larger pot).

Follow the same procedure as for pricking out, using one container per seedling. Never use too large a one in the first place; if they are staying in pots increase the size as they grow, allowing them to build up a substantial root system.

Planting out

Don't put any plants out into the bed until you have hardened them off by gradually getting them used to outdoor conditions. Tender plants must not go out until all chance of frost has gone.

Plant them out into well-prepared ground, preferably when it is moist. Water the plants in the containers beforehand, make the hole with a trowel, put in the plant, replace the soil and firm it down with your fingers.

If the weather is particularly dry, puddle them in by making a hole, filling it with water, allowing it to soak in, planting and covering up with dry soil, to seal the moisture in.

Re-seal part-used packets of seeds and store them in a dry place or in the salad drawer of the fridge.

• 5 •
Cuttings Outdoors

You can root quite a number of cuttings very easily outdoors. All you need is a small piece of well-drained ground, a window box or a container about 13 cm (5 in) deep, filled with an open, gritty, well-drained soil-based compost. The only tools you will need are a sharp pair of secateurs, a knife, a dibber, a quantity of sharp sand and a hormone rooting agent.

HARDWOOD CUTTINGS

Most of our shrubs, fruit bushes and some trees are best propagated by taking hardwood cuttings. These are lengths of the current season's healthy growth, when the stem has begun to ripen at the end of the season.

The best time to take them is mid to late autumn. Select pieces the thickness of a pencil, mature enough so that when you try to bend them there should be very little 'give'. Normally, a cutting of this type is 20–23 cm (8–9 in) long, but they can vary, depending on the plant from which they are taken.

Some stems have buds positioned quite close together, whilst others are spaced well apart. Each cutting should carry at least three buds.

You can prepare several cuttings from one piece of stem if it happens to be long enough, but discard the end if it is too thin.

If you do any autumn pruning the branches you cut off can be a good source of material. When taking them from the parent, always cut just above a bud and one that is facing in the direction you wish the tree or shrub to grow the following season.

Prepare the cutting by making a good, clean straight cut from just below a bud at the base and by making a slanting one immediately above a bud at the top (Fig. 11a). This will ensure that you insert your cuttings the right end up.

Deciduous plants

If any of the cuttings still have leaves attached, remove them before planting. It also makes for easier, safer and less painful handling if spines are removed from prickly stems, but do it carefully so that you don't damage or tear the bark.

• *Roses* You can increase the number of roses you have by taking this type of cutting and, as it can be done at the end of the flowering season, it should not spoil the display. Choose the healthiest looking stems that you have cut off and use these.

Ramblers, climbers and quite a lot of the shrub roses root quite readily, the Hybrid teas (large-flowered) and the Floribundas (cluster-flowered) can be a little more difficult. Those with the darker stems from the strongest growing varieties are the easiest to root, but it's worth trying any of them. If you find them difficult, take twice as many as you need.

· HANDY TIP ·

If space is limited, tie several hardwood cuttings in a bundle and plant them in a trench lined with sand. When they have rooted, separate them and line them out in a nursery bed or pot them singly.

The resultant plants will not be as strong growing as those budded onto briar stocks, they will not grow as tall and may not be as long lived. But their one big advantage is that they will not send up any suckers. Every bit of growth they produce will be of the rose itself.

Evergreens

Several evergreens can also be propagated using hardwood cuttings, but you only remove any leaves that would be buried or come in close contact with the soil. If these are left on they will rot and cause damage.

Buds

Buds are usually left on the cutting, but there are a few exceptions such as red and white currants, gooseberries and one or two ornamentals. These benefit from being grown on a short leg – a short piece of bare trunk above ground before allowing any branches to form. A 23 cm (9 in) length of stem of any of these plants will carry numerous buds. Remove the bottom ones, leaving the top three or four, which will eventually form the branches.

Preparing the soil

Choose a sunny, sheltered spot in the garden and dig it over, removing any weeds as you go. Add large amounts of grit to heavy soil to prevent it from holding too much water and becoming

Fig. 11 Rooting hardwood cuttings outdoors.

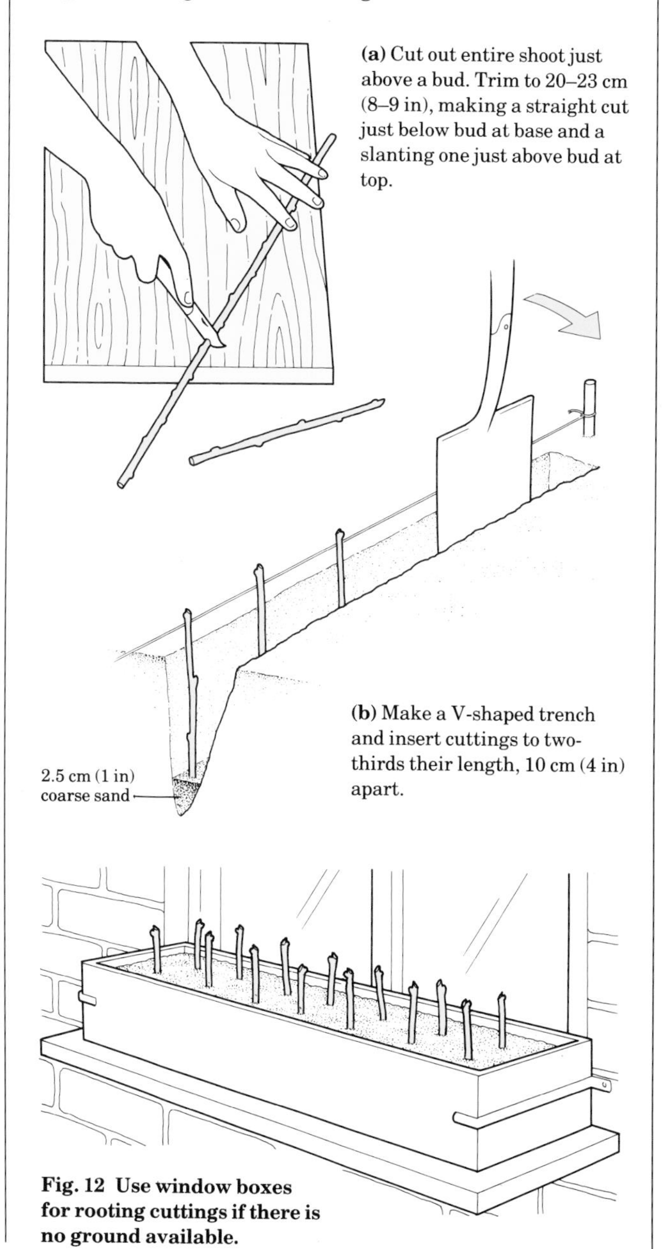

Fig. 12 Use window boxes for rooting cuttings if there is no ground available.

waterlogged, or add moist peat or well-rotted garden compost if the ground is light and sandy, as this will help it to retain moisture if the weather is dry. Level it, firm it by trampling it down with your feet. Then using a line as a guide, push the spade in to make a slit trench 18 cm (7 in) deep or a little deeper for long cuttings. Pull the spade towards you to make an opening which is wider at the top than the bottom so that one side is vertical and the other slanting (Fig. 11b). In the base of the V add 2.5 cm (1 in) of coarse sand, (not soft, builder's sand), to aid rooting and improve drainage.

Inserting the cuttings
Each cutting should be rested firmly on the sand with two thirds of it buried below ground. They can be placed quite close together, as near as 10 cm (4 in), resting against the straight side of the trench. Then push the soil back with your feet so that the cuttings are planted securely. If the ground is dry they will benefit from a good watering, which will also settle the soil and the sand around the base of each cutting.

• *Winter checks* Cuttings should be checked occasionally throughout the winter months, especially after frost or heavy rain. When it thaws it can lift and loosen them and then they should be pushed back gently and re-firmed with your feet. After a heavy downpour soil can be washed away from around them. Replace it as soon as possible and press it down hard.

Rooting
Hardwood cuttings take quite a long time to produce roots. Even if they put on new growth in the spring it does not necessarily mean that any have been formed. Don't be tempted to lift them for at least twelve months. After that, try one or two and if any roots have been formed, they can be moved and lined out in a nursery bed or potted up singly into 13 cm (5 in) pots, to be planted out in a further twelve months' time.

ROOT CUTTINGS

Some of our most hardy, vigorous plants can be multiplied by taking root cuttings outdoors in late autumn. Raspberries, blackberries, loganberries etc. and trees such as poplars. The tree of Heaven (*Ailanthus altissima*), the sumac tree (*Rhus typhina*) and rose briars which are to be used for budding, can all be prepared this way.

Method
Prepare the ground as above and cut the roots, which should be 6–13 mm (¼–½ in) thick, into 10 cm (4 in) lengths. Lay them horizontally in a shallow trench covered with 2.5 cm (1 in) of soil. Press it down firmly, water it and the following spring green shoots will appear above the ground, but it will be autumn before they will be ready for lifting. Do check that they are ready before lifting them all. They can then be potted or planted in a nursery bed until large enough to plant out.

When lifted, you may find that some of them will have produced more than one shoot, each with its own root system. You can either discard the weakest growths, leaving just one, or you can cut the old root in half and use both of them.

OTHER OUTDOOR CUTTINGS

Tender perennials
Geraniums (zonal pelargoniums) and some of the other tender perennials can be rooted outdoors during mid-summer. The best cuttings are taken

▶ *Rosa* 'New Dawn' is a good example of a climber that roots readily from hardwood cuttings.

from non-flowering shoots so that you do not spoil the summer display. Quite often you will find that every one is carrying flowers or buds and then they have to be used.

The final cuttings should be 8–10 cm (3–4 in) in length. When they have been removed from the parent plant make a clean cut just below a joint, remove the bottom leaves, the stipels and any buds or flowers, so that when the cutting is planted none of the leaves touch the soil.

• *Method* Dig over a small area of ground which is in good light, but out of full sun. Clear it of weeds and if it is heavy add grit for extra drainage. Rake it level, tread it down firmly, rake it again and then spread a 2.5 cm (1 in) layer of sharp sand over the whole area. This also needs firming with the back of a spade or a board.

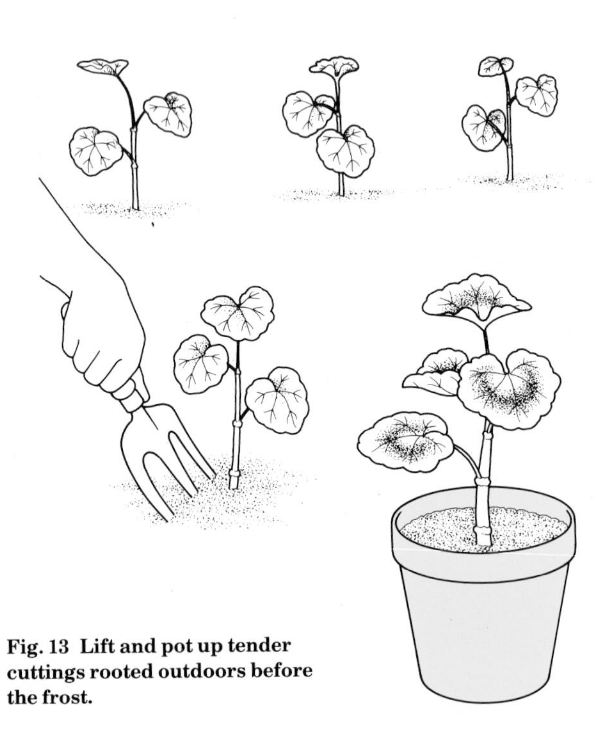

Fig. 13 Lift and pot up tender cuttings rooted outdoors before the frost.

• *Planting the cuttings* Insert the prepared cuttings 10 cm (4 in) apart, leaving 15 cm (6 in) between each row. You will find a small dibber ideal for this job as they must not be planted too deep – about one third of the stem should be below ground. Make sure that they are firmly planted and water them in using a fine rose to settle them. Don't give them too much water. The sand may look dry, but underneath the soil can be quite moist. They will only need extra water if we get a prolonged dry period. If they are too wet they will rot.

• *Winter protection* Because they are not fully hardy these cuttings must not stay outdoors during the winter. Before the weather turns cold, lift them and pot them up separately into 9 cm (3½ in) pots, using a John Innes No.1 potting compost with a little extra grit added for better drainage (Fig. 13).

They must be kept in good light and frost free. A temperature of between 7–10°C (45–50°F) will be ideal. Be careful with the watering, as more of these cuttings are lost by giving them too much than by keeping them on the dry side.

If you have rooted your cuttings in a container, it can be lifted under cover without disturbing them and they can be potted up separately in the spring.

House plants

Quite a number of house plant cuttings can be rooted outdoors, such as small-leaved ivies, fatshedera, *Fatsia japonica*, cissus and any others that like cool conditions.

Take 10 cm (4 in) long cuttings from the tips of the shoots early in the summer, cutting them just below a joint. Remove the bottom leaves and treat with hormone rooting powder. This will give them plenty of time to root so that they can be potted before the weather turns cold.

· 6 ·
Cuttings Under Glass

Only take cuttings from healthy, vigorous stock as every one will grow exactly like its parent, even when it comes to disease. If you have several of a variety, only propagate from the best one.

SOFTWOOD CUTTINGS

These are pieces of young stems with leaves and a growing point, taken before the stem starts to ripen. House plants and many tender perennials are propagated in this way.

Correct conditions

Softwood cuttings need warmth and humidity and shading from the sun if they are to root successfully. The best time to take them is from mid-winter until late summer, whenever the shoots are a suitable length.

They will root quite easily on a light, north-facing window sill in a warm room; one above a radiator would be ideal. If you have a heated propagator that will maintain a temperature of 16–18°C (60–65°F) on a well-lit window sill, in a greenhouse or a conservatory, you will get even better results.

Method

Select healthy shoots, approximately 13 cm (5 in) long and cut them from the plant just above a joint. Trim them to 8 cm (3 in), cutting cleanly through the stem immediately below a leaf joint with a sharp knife, leaving no snags and taking care not to bruise them. If they are not being used straight away, place them in a clean, sealed plastic bag to stop them wilting. Trim the leaves from the bottom third of the stem, as any buried in the compost will rot.

You only need to take cuttings 4 cm (1½ in) long from some plants such as fuchsias and then you strip half the stem of leaves.

Most softwood cuttings root quicker if they are treated with a hormone rooting agent. Only put it on the bottom 6 mm (¼ in) and if it is powder, be sure to remove any excess.

Fill a pot or tray with a well-drained compost, firm it, water it and allow it to drain. Make holes with a small dibber and insert the cuttings to one third their length. They should sit on the compost in the bottom of the hole; if they are in an air pocket they will not root. Firm the compost around the stems, water them again and place them in a temperature of 16–18°C (60–65°F). The air should be moist, so place a glass or plastic cover over them.

Basal cuttings

Basal cuttings are taken from plants such as chrysanthemum that provide new growth from their roots and tuberous plants which produce new shoots from old tubers. Cut them off when the shoots are 10–13 cm (4–5 in) long and treat them as other softwood cuttings.

SEMI-HARD CUTTINGS

These are taken from the current year's growth, just as the stems start to harden but whilst the tips are still quite soft, so are half way between softwood and hardwood. They are found at the end of side growths or at the top of the main shoot. Quite a large number of deciduous and evergreen shrubs and outdoor climbers are propagated in this way.

- *Nodal cuttings* are usually taken from deciduous trees and shrubs in early summer.
- *Heel cuttings* are particularly suitable for evergreen subjects and conifers and should be taken between mid-summer and mid-autumn.

Semi-hard cuttings are prepared in a very similar way to softwood cuttings, but in most cases they

▲ Heather cuttings are very small so a 13 cm (5 in) pot will hold quite a number.

◀ Nodal cuttings are taken by slicing cleanly through the stem just below a joint.

are longer, between 10–15 cm (4–6 in). There are exceptions – heathers, because of the way they grow, will only be about 4 cm (1½in) in length.

Nodal cuttings
These are short pieces of stem trimmed cleanly just below a joint with a sharp knife. Remove the bottom leaves and any flower buds, and the tip if it is very soft and fleshy.

Heel cuttings
Tear the young shoots away from the parent plant with a sliver of the older wood attached (this is the heel). Trim any ragged or thin pieces of bark, otherwise they may rot. Both types of cuttings will root quicker if you use a hormone rooting agent.

Fill a 13 cm (5 in) pot with cutting compost, press it down, add 3 mm (⅛ in) layer of sharp sand to the surface and firm it down. Plant the cuttings to one third of their length, firm and water them.

Conditions for rooting
Place the cuttings in a cold frame or cold greenhouse and keep the compost slightly on the dry side. For the first few days create a humid atmosphere by closing the frame tops or greenhouse vents and keep the glass shaded. Later, ventilate on warm days when temperatures rise above 18°C (65°F).

They can stay in their original container until the following spring when they should be potted up individually or lined out in a nursery bed.

Check the cuttings regularly for pests and diseases and take suitable action to control them. Remove any yellowing leaves and pick up any that have fallen.

• *House plants* Take semi-ripe cuttings of tender shrubs and climbers that are grown indoors or under glass. Use the same methods, but they will require a higher temperature of 18–21°C (65–70°F) to get them to root.

ROOT CUTTINGS

Some of these will root outdoors, but the majority will benefit from being placed under cover. Herbaceous plants which produce thick, fleshy roots are propagated this way and a few fibrous rooted ones such as perennial phlox. These cuttings are taken when the plants are dormant and when the ground is free of frost and not waterlogged.

Method
Lift small plants completely, shake off the soil to expose the roots and wash them if necessary so that you can see what you are doing.

If plants are too large to lift, dig a hole away from the base to expose one or two suitable roots. Choose young, vigorous ones if possible. The fleshy ones should be about as thick as a pencil and the fibrous ones similar to a shoelace (Fig. 14).

Lay the thicker roots on a board, noting which end was attached to the parent (this is the top). Remove any side growths and slice the main root into 8 cm (3 in) long sections, cutting the top end straight across and the bottom at an angle so that later you know which end up to plant them.

Fill a pot with cutting compost, press it down slightly, water it and allow it to drain. Treat all the wounds on the cuttings with a hormone rooting powder containing a fungicide. Make holes using a dibber 5 cm (2 in) apart and insert the cuttings so that the tops are level with the compost surface. Water to settle them in.

Cut the thin roots into 5 cm (2 in) long pieces, straight at both ends and seal with a hormone rooting powder. Place them horizontally on top of

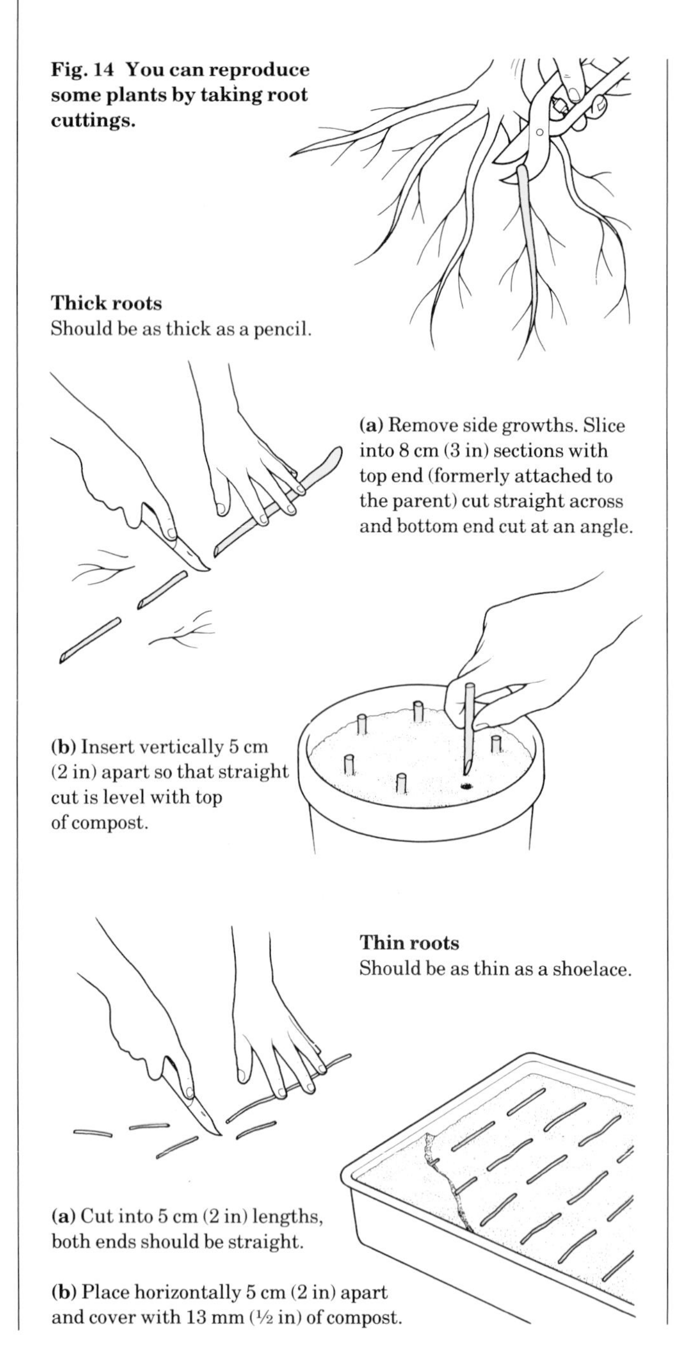

Fig. 14 You can reproduce some plants by taking root cuttings.

· HANDY TIP ·

Cut 10 cm (4 in) off the top of a clear plastic drinks bottle, complete with cap, and use it as an individual propagator on the top of a suitably sized pot. Remove the cap to ventilate once the cuttings have rooted.

the compost in a tray in rows 5 cm (2 in) apart and cover them with a 13 mm (½ in) layer of compost.

Place the containers in a cold frame, cold greenhouse or in a sheltered spot in the garden, covered with a cloche or a piece of glass weighted down and keep the compost just moist.

In spring, when the weather warms, new growth will appear, but give them time to produce a good root system before potting them up or lining them out.

Some less hardy shrubs such as ceanothus and convolvulus need a temperature of 16°C (60°F) to root. These should be placed in a heated propagator.

LEAF CUTTINGS (Fig. 15)

Plants with thick, fleshy leaves such as cape primrose (streptocarpus), gloxinia (sinningia) and mother-in-law's tongue (sanseveria) are increased by taking leaf cuttings. They will root at any time, but it is best to take them in spring or summer.

Method

Cut long, healthy leaves from the plant as near to the crown as possible. Slice them into 8 cm (3 in) lengths, cutting it cleanly and keeping each piece the right way up (the edge nearest the tip being the top). Treat the cut edges with hormone rooting powder and insert them 5 cm (2 in) apart into a pot or tray of cutting compost, burying about one third of them. Eventually, you will get one or two young plants appearing from the base of each piece of leaf.

- *Leaf cuttings of cape primroses* can be taken by cutting the leaf in half lengthways down the centre of the main vein, using a sharp blade. Treat both edges with a rooting agent and plant them 13 mm (½ in) deep, cut edge downwards. They can be curved if you are using a pot. Young plantlets will develop at intervals all the way along the bottom edge.

- *Leaves which have a stalk attached* such as African violets (saintpaulia) are the easiest to root. Select healthy, mature leaves and cut them, complete with stalk, neatly from the plant. Shorten the stem to approximately 2.5 cm (1 in) in length, using a sharp knife or razor blade. Dip the cut end in a hormone rooting agent and insert them into a container of cutting compost, using a dibber to make the holes. Make sure that the bottom of the stem is touching the compost in the bottom of the hole and that the leaf is sitting on the surface of the compost. Each leaf will produce several new growths.

- *The large leaves of plants such as Begonia rex* can be left whole. Make a 13 mm (½ in) long cut through all the main veins from which young plants will grow and lay it flat on moist compost. The piece of leaf where the veins are cut must be in contact with the compost, weighed down with small stones or pinned with U-shaped pieces of thin wire.

Alternatively they can be cut into small pieces the size of a postage stamp, but each one must have a piece of the main vein running through it. Insert these into the compost right end up, burying one third of their length.

Fig. 15 There are several ways of taking leaf cuttings. Use only healthy leaves that are neither too young nor too old.

(a) Streptocarpus (cape primrose)

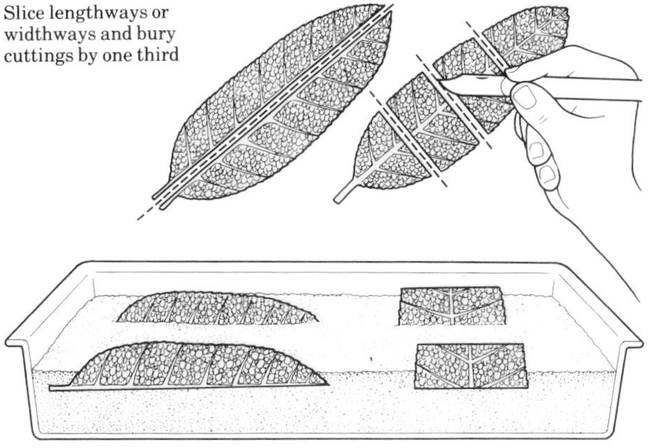

(b) Saintpaulia (African violet)

(c) Begonia

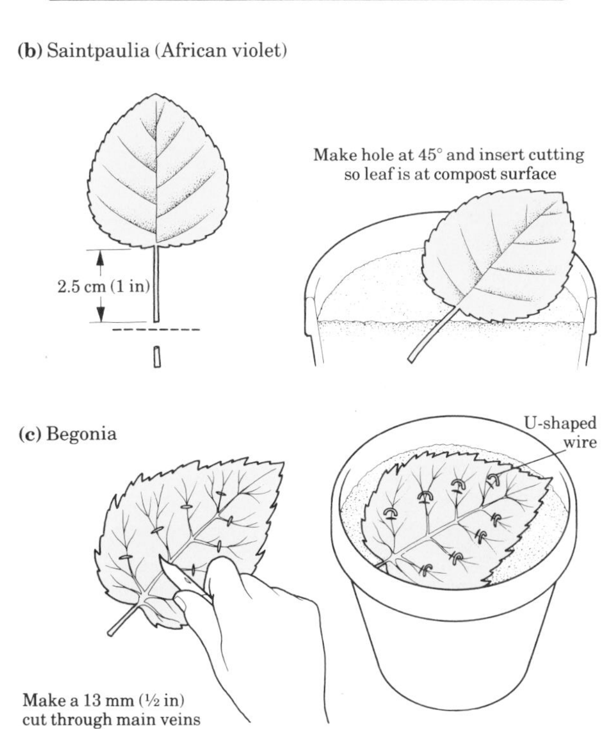

Conditions

Leaf cuttings require warm, humid conditions. After watering, place them in a heated propagator at a temperature of 16–18°C (60–65°F) or in an unheated propagator or covered with a polythene bag on a window sill in a warm room, but shaded from bright sunlight. They can take from six weeks to six months to root and produce young plantlets.

When the plantlets are large enough to handle without damaging them, tease them carefully out of the compost and away from the leaf. Pot them up separately into small pots of potting compost and put them back into the propagator until they become established.

· PLANTS PROPAGATED BY CUTTINGS ·

Basal cuttings		
Achillea	Delphinium	Nepeta
Anacyclus	Galega	Physostegia
Anaphalis	Gentian	Platycodon
Arenaria	Gypsophila	Pyrethrum
Armeria	Heliopsis	Scabious
Chelone	Lupin	Sidalcea
Chrysanthemum	Lychnis	Silene
Codonopsis	Lysimachia	Tanacetum
Cyananthus	Lythrum	Veronica
Dahlia	Malva	Viola
Root cuttings		
Ailanthus	Celastrus	Limonium
Anchusa	Clerodendrum	Marjoram
Aralia	Dendromecon	Mint
Arnebia	Dicentra	Oregano
Bergenia	Echinacea	Phlox
Brunnera	Echinops	Physalis
Campsis	Embothrium	Pulsatilla
Catalpa	Erodium	Romneya
Catananche	Eryngium	Sorbaria
Ceanothus	Geranium	Stokesia
Leaf cuttings		
Begonia	Saintpaulia	Streptocarpus
Peperomia	Sanseveria	Succulents

LEAF-BUD CUTTINGS

These consist of a leaf with a piece of stem attached and a healthy growth bud in the axil (where the leaf and the stem meet). Several hardy and indoor plants can be propagated this way.

Take cuttings from hardy plants in late summer/early autumn. A length of healthy growth will provide several cuttings. Cut just above a bud at the top and leave 2.5 cm (1 in) of stem below. Apply a hormone rooting agent to the wounds and plant them firmly in a container of cutting compost with the bud resting on the surface.

Tie cuttings with large leaves to a small cane to keep them stable. Or you can reduce the leaf area by cutting them in half.

They will root in a cold frame, but then you will have more success if you give them bottom heat.

● *Cuttings of indoor plants such as rubber plants* (*Ficus elastica*) are taken in a similar way in spring or early summer. Cut the stem into 2.5 cm (1 in) sections with a leaf and bud attached. Apply hormone rooting powder to both ends to prevent them bleeding. Roll the large leaves and hold them in position with an elastic band and support them by tying them loosely to a short split cane. Place them in a temperature of 16–18°C (60–65°F) in a propagator, or similar place, where the atmosphere is warm and humid.

All leaf-bud cuttings are better rooted separately in 9 cm (3½ in) pots so that you need not disturb them until they are well established. They will need potting on into a larger pot when the original one becomes full of roots.

► Plants such as saintpaulia which produce leaf stalks can be propagated by taking leaf cuttings, as shown in Fig. 15(b).

M&B

· 7 ·
Division

This is the easiest and most successful way of increasing your stock of plants. Most herbaceous perennials, many alpines, several aquatic plants and one or two shrubs are increased by this method and a large number of house plants can be divided when they become pot bound.

SIMPLE DIVISION

Digging up plants from the soil and then splitting them into several pieces, all with roots attached, is the simplest way to carry out division (Fig. 16). There is very little skill involved although it should be done at the correct time of year.

Michaelmas daisies (perennial asters), polyanthus, primroses and scabious grow in clumps and can be divided quite easily.

Water lilies and several other plants that grow in ponds need dividing every now and again if they are to flower year after year.

Shrubs that produce new shoots from below ground but very close to the parent can be lifted, pulled apart and the small pieces replanted to grow on and mature.

Suckers from such as raspberries can be dug up and used to increase stock.

Timing

The best time of year to divide plants is either in the autumn, when they are going dormant and the ground is still warm, or in spring, just as the new shoots are emerging. This will vary from area to area and year to year, depending on the weather. But like all other methods of propagation, some plants behave differently and need to be divided at other times of the year.

Pyrethrums (*Tanacetum coccineum*) normally bloom in early summer. If these were divided in spring they would not have put on very much

· EASILY DIVIDED PLANTS ·

Plants which can be divided by hand without using tools.

Achillea	Cotula	Limonium
Aegopodium	Dicentra	Linaria
Agapanthus	Doronicum	Mimulus
Ajuga	Epimedium	Nepeta
Alchemilla	Erigeron	Nierembergia
Alstroemeria	Erinus	Omphalodes
Anaphalis	Erodium	Phlox
Androsace	Fragaria	Potentilla
Anthemis	Gentiana	Primula
Arenaria	Geranium	Pulmonaria
Armeria	Geum	Pyrethrum
Asperula	Glechoma	Saponaria
Astilbe	Helenium	Sedum
Astrantia	Hepatica	Sempervivum
Brunnera	Heuchera	Silene
Campanula	Inula	Sisyrinchium
Cerastium	Lamium	Trollius
Convallaria	Leontopodium	Veronica
Corydalis	Lewisia	Viola

growth by that time and so would not be large enough to flower. If the plants are cut back immediately after flowering they will then send up new shoots. When these are 13 cm (5 in) high they can be lifted and split.

Spring-flowering primulas and many iris behave in a similar way and these are also divided after the flowering period.

Early-flowering bulbs die down and go fully dormant after they have flowered in spring. These are best dug up in mid-summer, separated and replanted, ready for flowering the following year.

OFFSETS

Many plants we grow produce young shoots or bulbs, which are called offsets, around the parent. These are all new plants with roots and a crown. When separated from the main plant and potted up or planted out, they will grow and flower within two or three years. When they reach maturity they too will produce offsets.

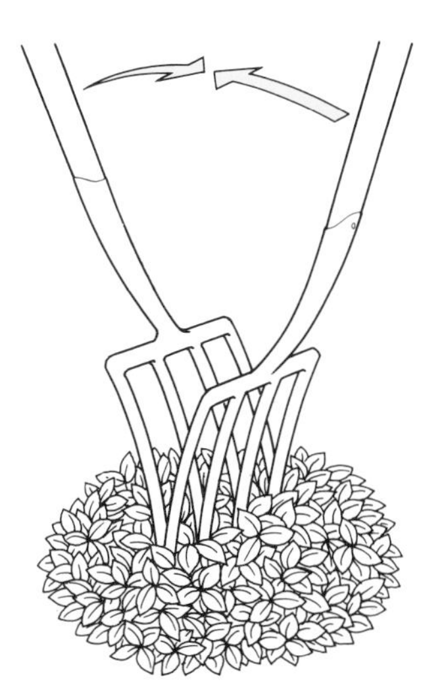

Fig. 16 Split fibrous-rooted herbaceous plants by placing two forks back to back and prising them apart.

· HANDY TIP ·

When lifting and dividing mature clump-forming herbaceous perennials, it is important that you only use the young, vigorous sections from the outside of the clump as these will make the best plants. Discard the old, woody centre.

The friendship plant (*Billbergia nutans*) will push up several new plants every year. Others such as the urn plant (*Aechmea fasciata*) will only form offsets once the old plant has flowered and starts to die.

A large number of cacti and succulents produce new offsets every year, as do bulbs and corms. When we take a rooted cutting from an herbaceous plant, this is also known as an offset.

SUCKERS

These are young growths which are produced from the roots around trees, shrubs and several fruit trees and bushes. When plants are growing on their own root systems, any suckers that they produce can be used for propagation purposes.

They can be taken off in autumn or early spring. Remove the soil by digging a hole around the young growth, taking care not to damage it or the parent tree. Bare the junction between it and the main root and, with a pair of sharp secateurs, loppers – or you may even need a saw if the root is thick – cut out the sucker with a short length of root attached. They then can be either potted up or planted out in a nursery bed to grow on for a few years.

Some suckers are quite large and will need supporting by tying them to a stake until they become established.

Even if you don't want them all, they should be removed by taking them away from the main root. If they are left they will rob the parent of valuable food.

Several plants, including roses, are budded or grafted onto various types of rootstocks. Suckers from these plants will be exactly the same as the stock, not the grafted plant. Remove these and discard them unless you want to propagate the rootstock for grafting and budding onto.

RHIZOMES

These are thick, swollen stems that grow horizontally from plants, either underground or very near the surface. Or, as in grasses, they may be thin and wiry. They contain growth buds and act as a food store for the young plants. But if they are broken or cut into small pieces containing one of these buds, they will grow and produce young plants. Bergenias, bamboos and many iris grow from these underground stems.

They are multiplied by cutting healthy rhizomes into sections carrying at least one or, better still, two or three buds. Some are quite happy planted outdoors, but certain ones require artificial heat to encourage them to grow. Several are divided in summer after flowering, others are best done during the winter months.

The iris that produces rhizomes will make very large clumps. The centre of these will die out and they will only produce leaves around the outer edge. Lift them every three or four years at the end of their flowering season. Dig them up and divide them into single rhizomes, using a strong knife if necessary. Retain the healthy ones with leaves attached and dispose of the old, woody ones from the centre. Reduce the length of the rhizomes to 8 cm (3 in) and the leaves by two thirds. Plant them in prepared ground so that the top of the rhizome is just showing above the surface and is facing the sun. Tie the leaves of each one to a small cane to give support until they have established themselves.

Lift bergenias in winter, remove one or two healthy, thick, fleshy roots (rhizomes) and replant them. Cut the roots into pieces 5 cm (2 in) long and dip them in a fungicide solution to prevent them from rotting. Plant them horizontally to half their depth in a tray of potting compost. Water them and place them in a heated propagator at a temperature of 21°C (70°F). Leave them until they have produced a good root system and then pot them into 10 cm (4 in) pots of potting compost. Keep them under cover for several weeks and then harden them off before planting them out in the borders.

◀ Many perennial plants are propagated by simple division, using two forks back to back to ease the roots apart.

▶ Propagate bergenias in winter by placing 5 cm (2 in) sections of the rhizomes/ roots in a 10 cm (4 in) pot of compost in a heated propagator.

TUBERS

Some plants such as dahlias, begonias and potatoes, produce these thick, swollen roots which they use as a food store, but they also provide us with another way of dividing them to increase our stock.

• *Dahlias* Dahlias can be multiplied by dividing a large tuber into sections, each containing one or more tubers and a piece of the old stem and, as along as it carries dormant buds, each one will produce a new plant (Fig. 17).

Plant the tubers in shallow boxes of compost in early spring, water them and place them in a temperature of 16°C (60°F) where they will produce shoots which can be used as cuttings.

Fig. 17 Increase your stock of dahlias by dividing the dormant tubers (a) *or* plant tubers in a box of compost (b) in late winter to produce young shoots for cuttings (c). Root the cuttings by inserting them in small pots of gritty compost.

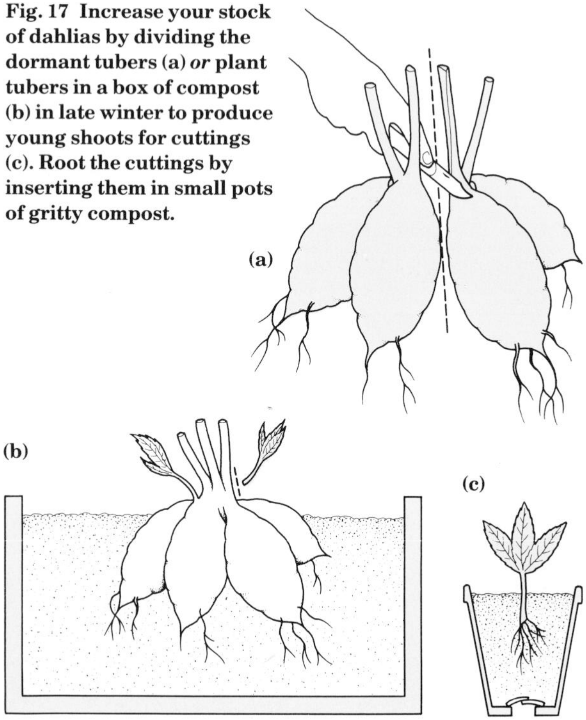

• *Begonias* Begonia tubers can be started into growth in early spring by planting them into a soil-less compost with their tops showing. If they are kept at a temperature of 16°C (60°F), keeping the compost moist, in a few weeks they will produce pink, dome-shaped buds. Then lift the tubers and cut them into pieces, each with at least one bud attached. Treat the wounds with a fungicide, pot them into 8 cm (3 in) pots of universal compost and keep them warm and in light. Each one will eventually grow into a flowering plant. The cut surfaces will not produce roots, so the plants will not be as vigorous as those growing from complete tubers. Left uncut, the tubers will produce shoots from which cuttings can be taken.

• *Potatoes* A seed potato is a tuber saved from the previous year's harvest which is then stored, sprouted and planted to produce another crop. The buried stem will develop underground roots on which the new tubers are formed. It is always advisable to buy Certified Disease Free stock to avoid spreading disease.

BULBS

Daffodils, narcissi, hyacinths, tulips, snowdrops etc. grow from bulbs. They multiply themselves by dividing or by producing small bulbs (often called bulbils, bulblets or offsets) around the base of the parent. These can take up to four years to reach flowering size.

Those left in the ground form large clumps and eventually the bulbs become closely packed together. When this happens they should be lifted in summer when dormant and divided, replanting the larger ones in their flowering positions. The smaller bulbils go into a nursery bed to grow on for a year or two to allow them to increase in size

· HANDY TIP ·

Remove scales from around the outside of lily bulbs, place them in a polythene bag of moist, soil-less compost, hang them up in a warm place such as an airing cupboard and shake them daily. When they have produced roots, plant them in a seed tray of potting compost to grow on.

before lifting them and planting them where they will flower in a few years' time.

- *Lilies* (*Lilium*) produce bulbils around the old bulbs, but they will also produce them on the stems in the leaf joints. These can also be removed and used for propagation.

CORMS

Gladioli, crocuses and several other plants grow from corms. These are solid food stores and have one or more buds on the top. When planted, these grow into flowering stems and when they die they form new corms at the bottom of each stem, on top of the old corm which, in time, shrivels and rots.

They also develop cormlets (otherwise known as cormels, spawn or offsets) and these are formed around the base of the mature corm.

After drying, remove them from the parent and store them dry through the winter. In early spring plant them, pointed end uppermost in a tray of potting compost 13 mm (½ in) deep and 2.5 cm (1 in) apart. The following autumn lift them, dry them and store them. Plant them the coming spring 8 cm (3 in) apart, 2.5 cm (1 in) deep, water and feed them and repeat the process for another season. Then they should be large enough to flower and can be planted outdoors.

Fig. 18 Plants divide themselves by a variety of methods.

Offsets
Amaryllis, Cacti, *Caladium*, *Clivia*, *Eucomis*, *Gloriosa*, *Haemanthus*, *Hippeastrum*, *Sprekelia*, Succulents, *Tulipa*, *Zantedeschia*

Suckers
Ceratostigma, *Clerodendron*, *Cornus*, *Diervilla*, *Embothrium*, *Fatsia*, *Gaultheria*, Raspberry, *Rhus*, *Sanseveria*, *Sorbaria*, *Yucca*

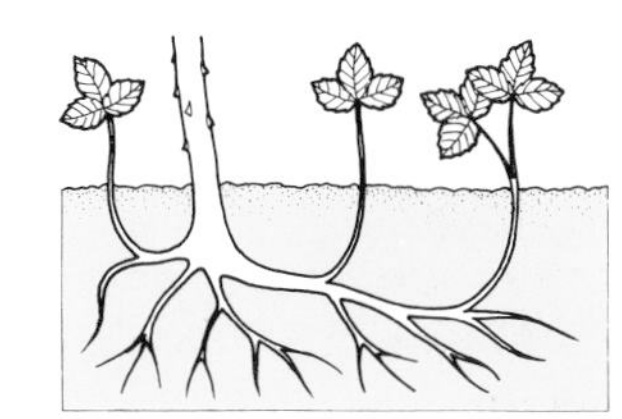

Rhizomes
Bergenia, *Canna*, *Clivia*, *Eremurus*, *Iris*, *Schizsostylis*

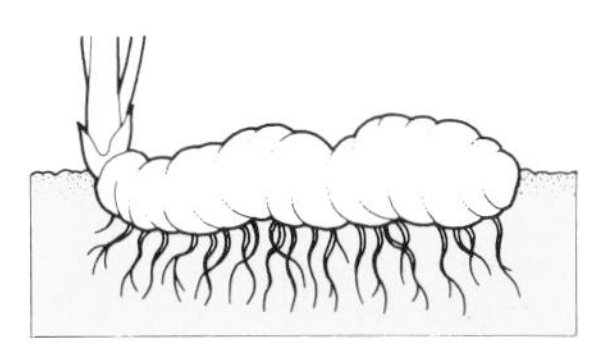

Tubers
Achimenes, *Anemone*, *Arum*, *Begonia*, *Dahlia*, *Eranthis*, Jerusalem artichoke, *Oxalis*, *Ranunculus*, *Sparaxis*, *Tropaeolum*

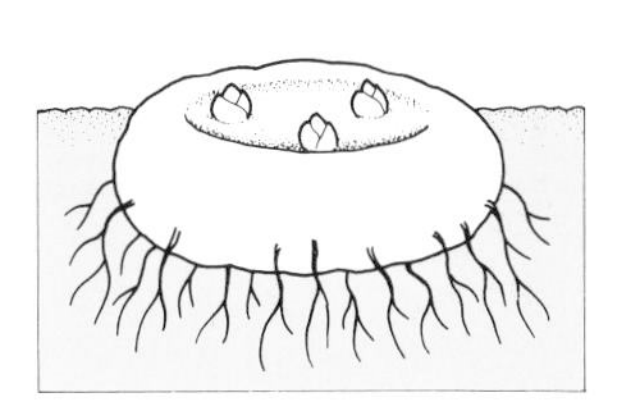

Bulbs
Allium, *Chionodoxa*, *Fritillaria*, *Galanthus*, *Hyacinth*, *Leucojum*, *Lilium*, *Muscari*, *Narcissus*, *Nerine*, *Scilla*, *Tulipa*

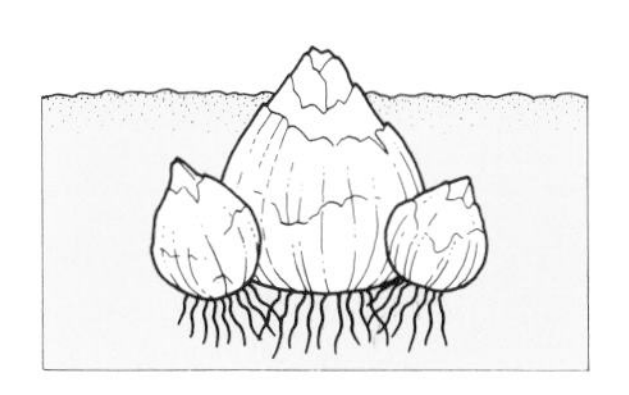

Corms
Acidanthera, *Anthericum*, *Crocosmia*, *Crocus*, *Freesia*, *Gladiolus*, *Ixia*, *Tritonia*

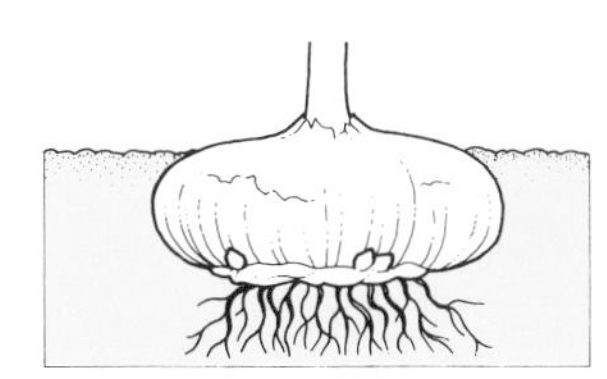

· 8 ·
Layering

Layering is a very easy and reliable way of increasing many trees and shrubs.

There are several different ways of layering, depending on the type of plant you are propagating and its habit. If a particular tree or shrub can't be propagated vegetatively any other way, always try layering it (Fig. 19).

SIMPLE LAYERING

You can imitate nature's way of layering as long as you can find a branch low or supple enough to reach the ground. This can be done at any time, but it is better to do it from early spring to late summer, whilst the plant is growing.

Ground preparation

Prepare the soil by forking it over and breaking down any lumps. If it is heavy it is a good idea to add a generous quantity of coarse sand to improve drainage and if it is free draining, incorporate well-rotted garden compost or peat to help moisture retention. Mix them thoroughly with the soil and firm it again.

Method

Choose a young, healthy stem, bend it down so that it touches the ground 30 cm (12 in) from the tip and mark the soil and the stem where the two meet. Strip off any leaves and side branches 10 cm (4 in) either side of this point and make an angled cut on the underside with a sharp knife, not quite half way through it. Place a sliver of wood into the cut to keep it open.

Bury the wounded part of the stem 8 cm (3 in) deep in a shallow hole with the growing tip facing upwards. Secure it with a U-shaped piece of strong wire to keep it in place, replace the soil and firm it down. Place a flat stone on top to conserve moisture and tie the protruding tip to a small cane to prevent it moving about.

Check it regularly, as the soil should be kept moist at all times and free from weeds.

It takes 12–18 months for enough roots to have formed before it can be severed from the parent. It will put on a spurt of growth when it has rooted and when this happens, use secateurs to cut through the stem between the plant and the rooted layer.

Leave it for a few months so that it gets used to fending for itself, then lift it and plant it.

TIP LAYERING

This type of layering is simple and is used for multiplying blackberries, loganberries and other related plants. This is best done in summer when it will root quickly.

Shrubs such as rhododendrons can be propagated quite easily by simple layering.

Tie the end of the shoot to a support to prevent the stem from moving in the soil.

Method

Take a strong, healthy, young shoot long enough to reach the ground. Prepare the soil in the same way as for simple layering. Dig a hole and bury the tip 13 cm (5 in) deep, making sure that the growing point is in contact with the soil in the bottom of the hole.

Tie the stem to a small cane to keep it in position. Replace the soil, firming it well and don't let it dry out.

A young shoot should appear by late autumn and this can then be cut free from the mother plant. Or you can wait until spring before lifting and replanting or potting.

SERPENTINE LAYERING

This is used for long-stemmed, climbing or creeping plants such as clematis, honeysuckle and jasmine. It is an extension of simple layering, but instead of producing just one new plant, you can get several, depending on the length of stem used.

Method

Select a pliable, healthy, vigorous young shoot. Lay it along the ground, not necessarily in a straight line and prepare the soil as before. When in position, parts of the stem will be buried in the ground and the sections between will be left exposed to form a row of arches. The new plants will emerge from each buried piece.

Take the leaves off every third or fourth leaf joint (node) and cut diagonally half way through the stem, just behind each one of these. Bury them 5–8 cm (2–3 in) deep, pegging them down, leaving at least two joints with leaves to form the arch above the ground.

(a) Simple layering.

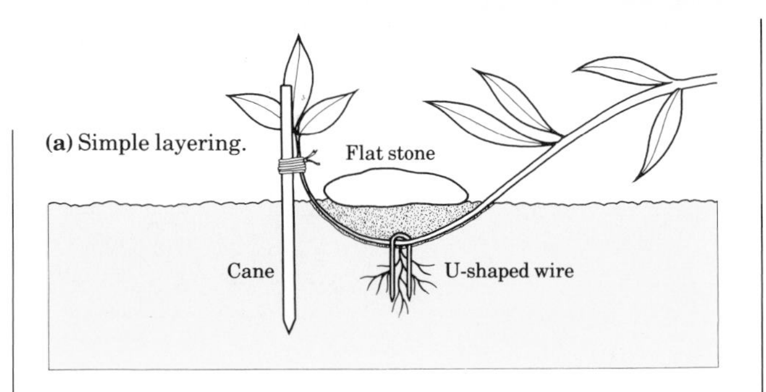

(b) Tip layering.

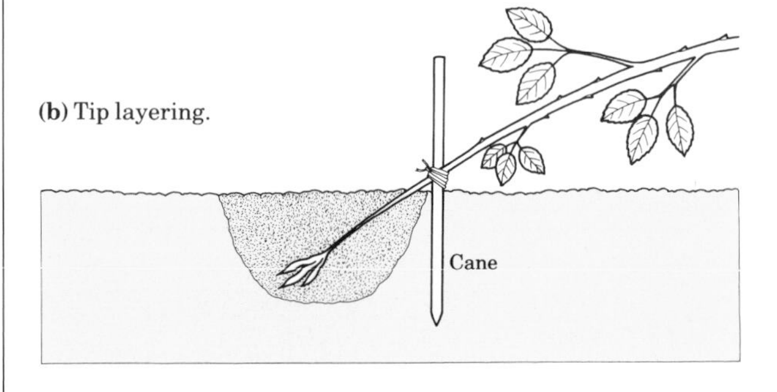

(c) Serpentine layering.

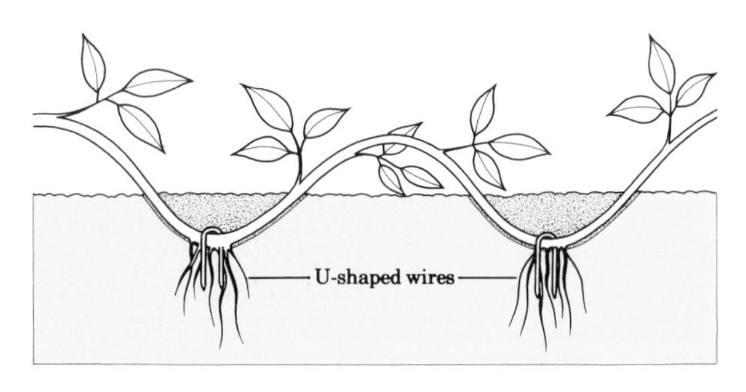

(d) Continuous layering.

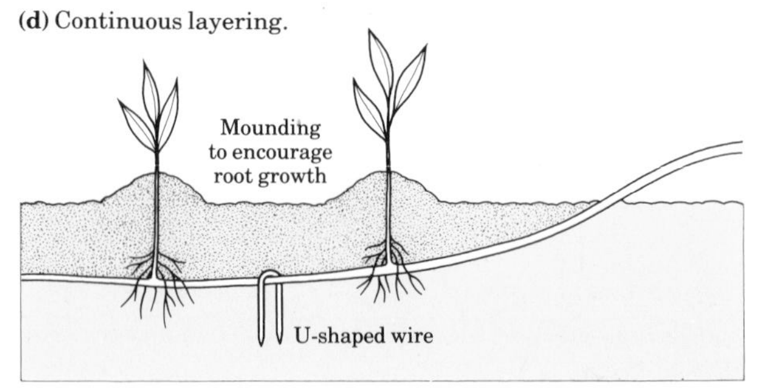

▶ **Fig. 19 Layering.**

They will take about 12 months to root and throw up shoots.

Lift them the following autumn, cut through the stem close to the roots on the side nearest the parent plant. Either plant them in a nursery bed or pot them up until they are large enough to plant out in their flowering positions.

If you prefer, you can layer using any of these three methods into pots of well-drained compost sunk in the ground.

CONTINUOUS LAYERING

Use this method to propagate shrubs which have long, slender stems such as the smoke bush (*Cotinus coggygria*). It is best carried out in the growing season.

Method

Use single-stemmed plants growing on their own roots. Bend the stem over gradually to avoid breaking it, and peg it down horizontally in a 5 cm (2 in) deep trench in prepared ground. Cover it, firm it and water it. Young shoots will appear along the stem. When they have grown a few inches in height, mound them up to encourage more roots. After about 18 months, lift them, cut them into sections, each with a shoot and roots attached, and pot them up or plant them in a nursery bed.

MOUND LAYERING

We sometimes refer to this type of layering as stooling. It is an effective way of propagating heathers, garden pinks etc, but it can also be used with a slight variation for gooseberries, black, red and white currants and other shrubs with upright-growing stems like the mock orange (*Philadelphus*).

Method

When they become straggly and woody, open them out in the centre and insert a mixture of equal quantities of sand, peat and soil to form a mound. This should be high enough and wide enough to cover all the mature parts of the stems and the base of the green shoots (Fig. 20). Firm down, water and add more of the mixture once it has settled.

If you do this in spring, the young shoots will root by the autumn. Lift the whole plant and cut away each single stem, complete with roots from the old plant. Pot them separately or plant them out.

Cut shrubs and fruit bushes hard back during winter and new shoots will appear in spring from around the base. When these have reached 15 cm (6 in) in height, mound soil around them so that the bottom 8 cm (3 in) of each young shoot is covered. By autumn these will have rooted and can be cut away from the parent. Plant them in a nursery bed and then into their final positions in 12 months time.

Fig. 20 Mound layering or 'stooling' (a) is an effective method of propagation for heathers and garden pinks. An alternative is dropping (b). Lift the plant and bury it deeper in the hole to encourage rooting.

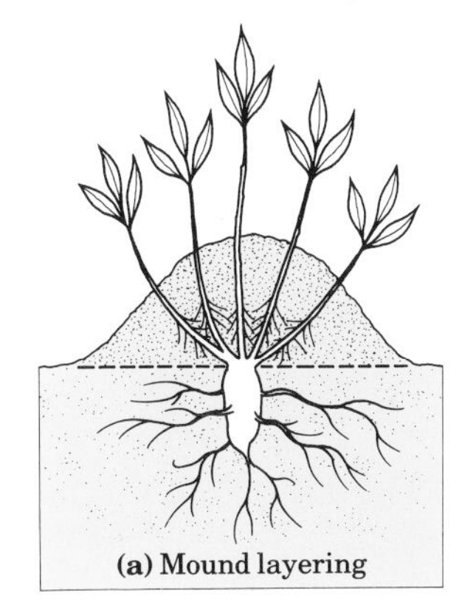

(a) Mound layering

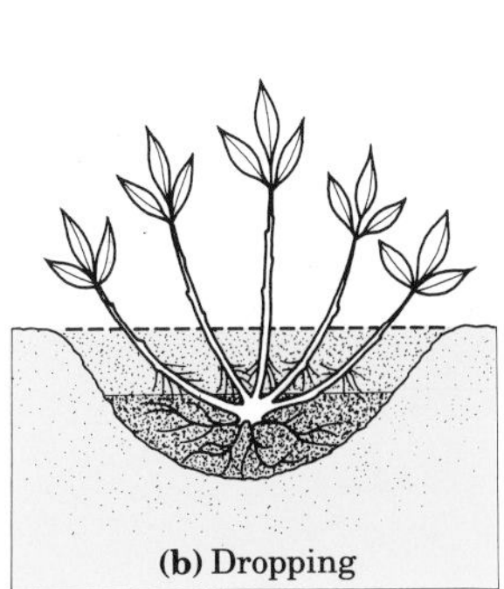

(b) Dropping

Air layering is a simple and convenient way to propagate rubber plants such as *Ficus elastica*.

AIR LAYERING

Quite a number of plants have stems that are too rigid or too short to bend and reach the ground. In this case, we have to take the rooting medium up to the branch and root it in mid air.

Many house plants are propagated in this way, but it can also be used quite successfully on hardy trees and shrubs.

Indoors or out the methods used are the same and should be carried out in spring or summer when the plants are producing new growth.

Method

Select a strong, healthy, young shoot and remove the leaf or leaves 30 cm (12 in) down from the tip. Make an upward-slanting cut, starting just below the leaf joint (node), cutting half way through the stem. Apply hormone rooting powder to the wound and wedge it open with a matchstick (a).

Coccoon the area with a wad of clean, damp sphagnum moss (b) and bind it with polythene, sealing the ends and joints to keep in the moisture (c). Use clear polythene to cover the moss when air layering. It will enable you to see when the roots have been formed without the need to remove it, which you would have to do when using black polythene.

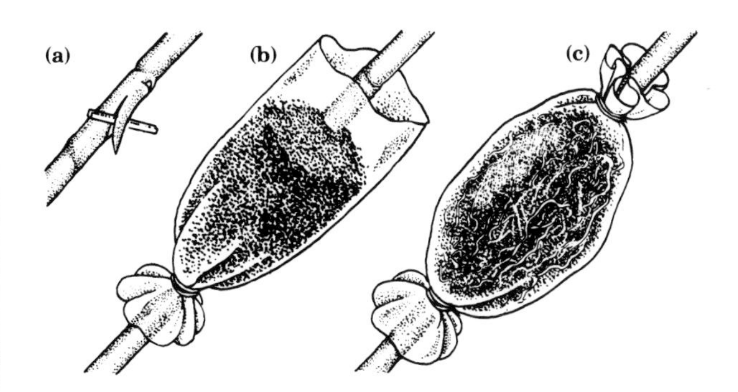

Fig. 21 Air layering of a rubber plant.

· PLANTS THAT CAN BE LAYERED ·

House and conservatory plants		
Acacia	Fatshedera	Monstera
Aphelandra	Ficus	Philodendron
Brunfelsia	Citrus	Schefflera
Dieffenbachia	Croton	
Shrubs		
Chimonanthus	Eucryphia	Paeonia
Cornus	Fatsia	Pieris
Cotinus	Magnolia	Rhododendron
Enkianthus		
Trees		
Acacia	Davidia	Mespilus
Acer	Garrya	Nyssa
Ailanthus	Halesia	Parrotia
Catalpa	Hoheria	Salix
Celtis	Itea	Stewartia
Cercis	Koelreuteria	Styrax
Corylus	Laburnum	Tilia
Crinodendron	Liriodendron	Ulmus

Or prepare the stem in the same way, take a 9 cm (3 in) pliable, plastic pot, cut down one side and across the base and cut out a circle to fit the stem snugly. When it is in position fill the pot with moist soil-less compost, making sure it is well pressed down and seal it with polythene.

Most indoor plants should have rooted in three to four months, but those outdoors will take 18–24 months. It is always best to check that good roots have formed by removing the polythene (which can be replaced if necessary) before cutting off the shoots just below where the roots have formed.

Remove any loose moss and pot up immediately in a well-drained potting compost. Those already in pots can be left for a few weeks and then potted on.

Place indoor plants in warm, humid conditions and those from outdoors in a cold frame or greenhouse.

· 9 ·

Problems with Seeds and Cuttings

Plants are vulnerable to attack by pests and diseases at any time, but they are even more at risk when they are small seedlings or cuttings before they have rooted. In fact it can prove fatal. In the warm, humid atmosphere of a propagator or in cold, damp conditions outdoors, they can spread very quickly and must be controlled at an early stage if precious seedlings and newly taken cuttings are to survive. Prevention is always better than cure, so strict hygiene is essential at all times.

SEED DRESSINGS

These are applied to seeds prior to them being sown. They can be either fungicides to control diseases or insecticides to deter insects, or they can be a combination of both.

Some seeds are very prone to attack, but these are usually treated by the seedsmen before they are despatched, and will be stated on the packet.

If you have trouble with certain types of seeds rotting off just before or after they have germinated, coating them with a seed dressing could solve the problem. Do be sure to read the instructions on the container first as they are not suitable for some seeds. Use it only as directed and just for the purpose for which it is intended.

SEEDLING ENEMIES

Viruses

These affect plants in many ways, causing them to become stunted or malformed. They could produce leaves which will curl, become crinkled or are not as wide as they should be, or they may be spotted or mottled with yellow. Stems may grow twisted or the whole plant may wilt. When flowers open they could be distorted and yields greatly reduced.

Viruses can be transmitted in the seed, but they are most likely to be moved from one plant to another in the sap. If insects feed by sucking the sap of an infected plant and then move on to a healthy one, they will transfer the virus.

When propagating vegetatively – taking cuttings, layering or dividing – if the parent plant is carrying a virus the new plants will too.

> **· SAFETY WITH CHEMICALS ·**
>
> Treat pesticides and fungicides with respect.
> - Store them in their original bottles.
> - Don't transfer them to other containers.
> - Always use them as directed.
> - Keep them out of the reach of children and pets.
> - Only use those approved for the amateur gardener.

You can even spread a virus from plant to plant when doing any type of pruning. Sap can be carried between plants on knives or secateurs. It's always as well to disinfect tools regularly.

The way to ensure that plants stay virus free is to keep them free from pests and only propagate from clean, healthy stock.

Insect pests

- *Aphids* (*greenfly*) spread virus diseases from one plant to another as they feed on the sap. Keep a watchful eye open for them indoors or out. They can be controlled in the greenhouse by fumigating and spraying, and outdoors by spraying. Take action at the first sign of attack, as one greenfly can produce several hundreds within a few weeks. You will find them mostly outdoors during the summer, but they are sometimes active during mild spells at other times of the year. In the confines of a greenhouse they can be found all the year round.

- *Woodlice* will nibble the leaves of young seedlings, limiting their growth. They will also attack small seedlings and they have been known to clear a container overnight within a few days of them germinating, leaving just small pieces of stalk sticking up out of the compost. They will suddenly take a liking for one kind of plant – it could be pansies and another time it could be petunias – they seem to have diet fads. You will find them lurking under boxes and pots on the greenhouse bench or under any debris that is left lying about. Being clean and tidy is a big help, but they can be controlled by putting down slug pellets which contain methiocarb or insecticide powders containing bendiocarb or HCH.

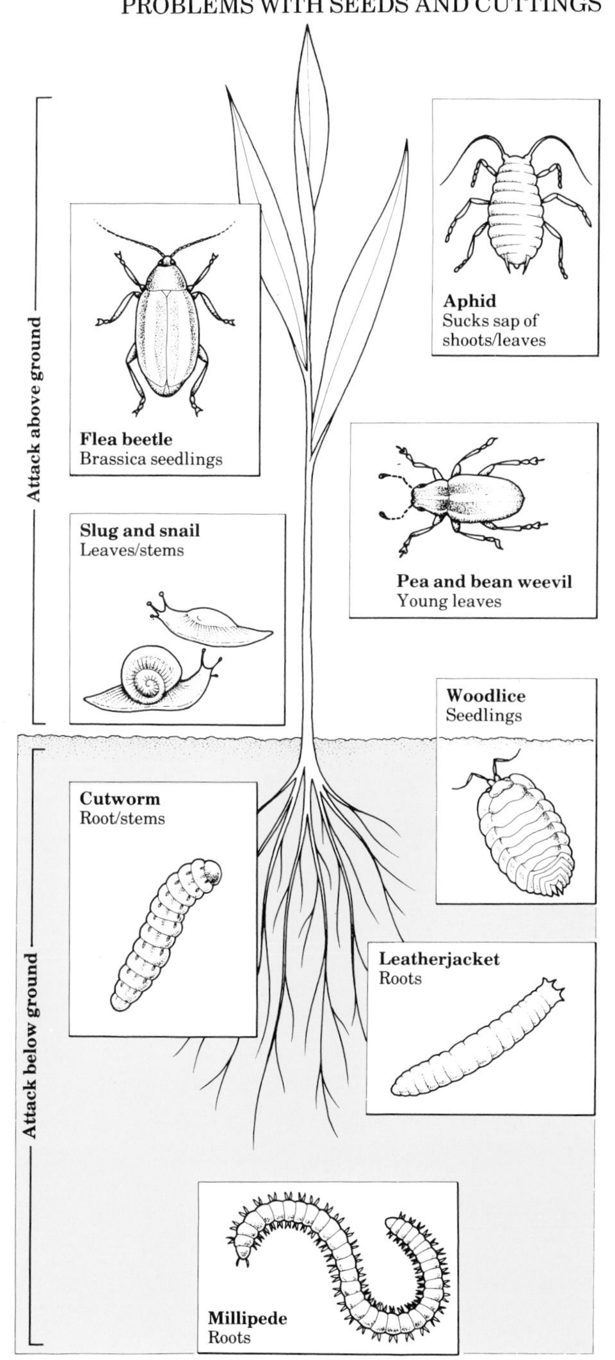

▶ Fig. 22 Some insects attack plants above ground, others feed on the roots.

• *Slugs and snails* are more likely to attack seedlings outdoors, but occasionally one or two will find their way into the greenhouse or cold frame. Use slug bait to control them, but if using pellets outdoors cover them with a piece of slate or a short length of upturned plastic guttering held in place with a piece of strong bent wire so that birds and pets can't reach them.

• *Flea beetles* attack young brassica seedlings by eating the edges of their leaves. Treat the seeds before you sow them with a seed dressing containing HCH or dust with a powdered insecticide along the rows of seedlings.

• *Pea and bean weevils* feed on the foliage of young seedlings, taking scallops out of the edges of the leaves and causing a check to growth. Apply a suitable insecticide dust to the soil along either side of the rows.

• *Cutworms* resemble greyish-brown caterpillars. They will eat through the stems of seedlings at soil level. One way of controlling them is to fork over the soil at regular intervals in winter, exposing them to the birds, and by applying a soil insecticide such as chlorophos around the young seedlings in spring.

• *Millipedes*, of which there are several different species, will eat into and destroy large seeds such as peas and beans and they will also damage the roots of seedlings. Use a seed dressing or dust along the open seed drills before sowing with a powder containing HCH.

• *Leatherjackets* are the larvae of crane-flies (sometimes better known as daddy-long-legs). They feed on seedlings' roots during autumn and spring. Disturb the soil in winter to bring them to the surface for the birds to eat or, if you prefer, apply a soil pest insecticide to the ground before sowing.

Diseases

• *Damping off* is the most common disease of seedlings and cuttings, causing them to collapse because the stems at soil level or the roots have rotted. The stems of cuttings will go black and they will die before they have rooted.

It can be quite common under cover, but it can also happen outdoors if plants are not given the correct conditions. In the greenhouse everything needs to be spotlessly clean. Wash every piece of equipment thoroughly using a garden disinfectant every time it has been used. Always use sterile or sterilized compost when sowing. Don't use compost more than once and never use soil straight from the garden. Prevent seedlings from becoming drawn through lack of light and never expose them to very high temperatures. Avoid sowing too thickly or the seedlings will be weak and spindly. When watering, use tap water; if for any reason rain water has to be used, make sure that all storage vessels are spotlessly clean – wash out and disinfect them at least once a year. They should have a lid on to keep out debris and light. Water emerging seedlings from below. If you water from above at this stage you could wash them into the compost and they will never recover.

At the first signs of any seedlings collapsing, remove them carefully, water the remainder with a copper-based fungicide and keep them on the dry side.

Outdoors it pays to rotate your crops as often as possible so that disease doesn't build up from one year to another in one part of the garden. Keep plants weed free and avoid using excessive amounts of high-nitrogen fertilizer. Never sow seeds when the soil is cold and wet. It is better to wait until the weather improves and the ground warms up.

When growing tomatoes, sow seeds thinly, as over-crowded seedlings are likely to damp off.

• *Club root* is a soil-borne fungus which attacks all members of the brassica family. It causes their roots to become swollen and knobbly and plants don't develop as they should. Once soil has become infected, it will remain so for many years.

It can be spread on soil attached to plant roots, on tools, footwear or in garden compost. So any plants carrying the disease should be destroyed, not added to the compost heap.

Unfortunately there is no cure, so it's important to keep soil clear. Always raise your brassica plants from seed. Don't buy in any open-rooted plants or accept them as gifts. Whenever you are going to grow this type of plant, check the pH. It should be pH 7 – neutral – or just above.

You can grow brassicas on infected ground, but restrict them to this part of the garden, don't rotate. Lime the soil heavily between each crop and raise the seedlings in individual 10 cm (4 in) pots of sterilized compost. Then soak the holes and the root balls in a systemic fungicide before planting them out. This won't give you a perfect crop, but at least it will allow you to grow cabbages, cauliflowers etc.

· 10 ·
Trees and Shrubs

The most common garden trees, shrubs, conifers and climbers have been assembled here, in an A–Z format, by the Latin generic name, for at-a-glance reference on the best methods of propagation. All of the techniques referred to in the lists that follow are explained fully in the earlier chapters.

Abelia S
Semi-ripe heel cuttings at 18°C (65°F) or cold frame in late autumn.
Abies (silver fir) C
Sow seeds outdoors in early spring.
Abutilon (Indian mallow) S
Sow seeds at 18°C (65°F) in early spring. Semi-ripe cuttings at 18°C (65°F) in mid to late summer. Hardwood cuttings in cold frame mid to late autumn.
Acacia (wattle) T/S
Scald seeds and sow at 24°C (75°F) in spring. Semi-ripe heel cuttings at 18°C (65°F) in summer.
Acca S
Sow seeds at 16°C (60°F) in spring. Semi-ripe heel cuttings at 16°C (60°F) in summer. Simple layering in summer.
Acer (maple) T
Sow seeds in cold frame or outdoors in autumn.
Aesculus (horse chestnut) T/S
Sow seeds outdoors in autumn.

KEY:
T = Tree C = Conifer
S = Shrub Cl = Climber

Ailanthus (tree of Heaven) T
Sow seeds in cold frame or outdoors in late winter/early spring. Root cuttings in cold frame in winter.
Akebia Cl
Semi-ripe cuttings at 18°C (65°F) in late summer/early autumn. Simple layering in summer.
Albizia T/S
Sow seeds at 21°C (70°F) in spring.
Alnus (alder) T/S
Sow seeds outdoors in autumn. Simple layering in summer.
Amelanchier (snowy mespilus) T/S
Sow seeds in cold frame or outdoors in mid-autumn. Simple layering in late spring. Remove rooted suckers in autumn.
Aralia T/S
Sow seeds outdoors in spring. Root cuttings in cold frame in winter.
Araucaria (monkey puzzle) C
Sow seeds at 16°C (60°F) in spring.
Arbutus (strawberry tree) T
Sow seeds in cold frame in spring. Simple layering in summer.
Aucuba (spotted laurel) S
Sow seeds in cold frame or outdoors in autumn. Semi-ripe cuttings in cold frame in early autumn. Simple layering in mid autumn.

Azara S
Semi-ripe cuttings at 18°C (65°F) in late summer. Hardwood cuttings outdoors in late autumn.
Berberis (barberry) S
Sow seeds outdoors in autumn. Semi-ripe heel cuttings in cold frame in early autumn.
Betula (birch) T
Sow seeds outdoors in autumn.
Buddleja (butterfly bush) S
Semi-ripe heel cuttings in cold frame in summer. Hardwood cuttings in cold frame in late autumn.
Buxus (box) S
Cuttings in cold frame in late summer/early autumn.
Callicarpa (beauty berry) S
Sow seeds at 16°C (60°F) in spring. Semi-ripe cuttings at 18°C (65°F) in summer.
Callistemon (bottle brush) T/S
Sow seeds at 18°C (65°F) in spring. Semi-ripe heel cuttings at 18°C (65°F) in summer.
Calluna (heather) S
Sow seeds when ripe in cold frame in autumn. Semi-ripe heel cuttings in cold frame in summer.
Camellia S
Sow seeds at 16°C (60°F) or outdoors

in autumn. Semi-ripe heel cuttings at 18°C (65°F) in late summer. Leaf bud cuttings at 21°C (70°F) in summer. Simple layering in late summer.
Campsis (trumpet vine) Cl
Sow seeds at 16°C (60°F) in spring. Semi-ripe cuttings at 18°C (65°F) in summer. Hardwood cuttings in cold frame in autumn. Root cuttings at 16°C (60°F) in winter.
Caragana (pea tree) T/S
Sow seeds outdoors in autumn. Semi-ripe cuttings at 18°C (65°F) in summer. Simple layering in summer.
Carpinus (hornbeam) T
Sow seeds outdoors in autumn.
Carya (hickory) T
Sow seeds in cold frame in autumn.
Caryopteris (bluebeard) S
Softwood basal cuttings at 18°C (65°F) in spring. Semi-ripe cuttings at 18°C (65°F) in summer.
Cassinia S
Semi-ripe heel cuttings in cold frame in autumn.
Cassiope S
Sow seeds in cold frame in spring. Semi-ripe cuttings at 16°C (60°F) in summer. Simple layering in summer.
Castanea (sweet chestnut) T
Sow seeds outdoors in autumn.
Catalpa (Indian bean tree) T
Sow seeds at 16°C (60°F) in spring. Semi-ripe cuttings at 18°C (65°F) in summer. Root cuttings in cold frame in winter.
Ceanothus S
Sow seeds at 16°C (60°F) in spring. Semi-ripe cuttings at 18°C (65°F) in summer. Root cuttings at 18°C (65°F) in early winter.
Celastrus (bittersweet) S
Sow seeds outdoors in autumn. Hardwood cuttings at 16°C (60°F) in autumn. Simple layering in summer. Root cuttings in cold frame in winter.
Celtis (nettle tree) T
Sow seeds at 16°C (60°F) in early spring. Hardwood cuttings in cold frame in late autumn. Simple layering in summer.
Cercis (Judas tree) T
Sow seeds at 16°C (60°F) in spring.
Chaenomeles (ornamental quince) S
Sow seeds in cold frame in autumn. Simple layering or semi-ripe heel cuttings at 16°C (60°F) in summer.
Chamaecyparis (false cypress) C
Sow seeds outdoors in early spring. Semi-ripe heel cuttings in cold frame in early autumn.
Chimonanthus (wintersweet) S
Sow seeds in cold frame in autumn. Simple layering in summer.
Chionanthus (fringe tree) T/S
Sow seeds outdoors in autumn. Simple layering in summer.
Choisya (Mexican orange blossom) S
Sow seeds in cold frame in spring. Softwood cuttings at 16°C (60°F) in early summer. Semi-ripe cuttings at 16°C (60°F) in autumn.
Cistus (rock rose) S
Sow seeds at 16°C (60°F) in spring. Semi-ripe cuttings in cold frame in summer.
Clematis (virgin's bower) Cl
Sow seeds in cold frame in autumn. Leaf bud cuttings at 18°C (65°F) in summer. Serpentine layering in summer.
Clerodendrum T/S
Semi-ripe cuttings at 18°C (65°F) in summer. Root cuttings in cold frame in winter. Suckers – remove and replant in spring.
Clethra (summer sweet) S
Sow seeds at 16°C (60°F) in spring. Semi-ripe heel cuttings at 18°C (65°F) in autumn.
Cordyline (cabbage palm) T
Sow seeds at 18°C (65°F) in spring. Cuttings of stem sections at 18°C (65°F) in summer.
Cornus (dogwood) T/S
Sow seeds at 16°C (60°F) in spring. Hardwood cuttings in cold frame or outdoors in autumn. Simple layering in summer. Suckers – remove and replant in spring.
Corokia S
Sow seeds at 16°C (60°F) in spring. Semi-ripe cuttings at 16°C (60°F) in autumn.
Coronilla (crown vetch) S
Sow seeds at 16°C (60°F) in spring. Semi-ripe cuttings in cold frame in autumn.
Corylopsis (winter hazel) S
Softwood cuttings at 18°C (65°F) in spring. Simple layering in summer.
Corylus (hazel) T/S
Sow seeds outdoors in autumn. Simple layering in summer.
Cotinus (smoke bush) T/S
Sow seeds in cold frame in autumn, Semi-ripe heel cuttings in cold frame in summer. Simple layering in autumn.
Cotoneaster S
Sow seeds in cold frame in autumn. Semi-ripe heel cuttings at 18°C (60°F) in summer. Simple layering in summer.
Crataegus (thorn) T/S
Sow seeds outdoors in autumn. Simple layering in summer.
Crinodendron (lantern tree) T
Semi-ripe heel cuttings at 16°C (60°F) in summer.
× **Cupressocyparis** (Leyland cypress) C
Semi-ripe heel cuttings in cold frame in late summer/early autumn.
Cupressus (cypress) C
Sow seeds outdoors in spring. Semi-ripe heel cuttings in cold frame in late summer/early autumn.

► Semi-ripe lavender heel cuttings should be taken in late summer, overwintered in a cold frame and transplanted to their flowering positions in spring.

► Hydrangea cuttings will root quite easily when taken in late summer.

► Opposite: The simplest way to propagate clematis is by serpentine layering.

Cytisus (broom) S
Sow seeds at 18°C (65°F) in spring. Semi-ripe heel cuttings at 16°C (60°F) in summer.
Daboecia (St. Dabeoc's heath) S
Sow seeds outdoors in autumn. Semi-ripe heel cuttings in cold frame in summer. Mound layer in spring.
Danae (Alexandrian laurel) S
Sow seeds outdoors in spring. Divide in spring.
Daphne S
Sow seeds outdoors in autumn. Semi-ripe cuttings at 18°C (65°F) in summer. Simple layering in spring/summer.
Davidia (handkerchief tree) T
Sow seeds outdoors in autumn. Semi-ripe heel cuttings at 18°C (65°F) in summer. Air layer in spring/summer.
Decaisnea S
Sow seeds in cold frame in autumn.
Decumaria Cl
Sow seeds in cold frame in autumn. Semi-ripe nodal cuttings at 16°C (60°F) in summer.
Dendromecon (tree poppy) S
Sow seeds at 16°C (60°F) in spring. Semi-ripe cuttings at 16°C (60°F) in summer. Root cuttings at 16°C (60°F) in winter.
Desfontainia S
Sow seeds at 18°C (65°F) in spring. Semi-ripe cuttings at 18°C (65°F) in late summer. Layer in late summer.
Deutzia S
Sow seeds in cold frame in autumn. Semi-ripe cuttings at 18°C (65°F) in summer. Hardwood cuttings in cold frame in autumn/winter.
Diervilla (Bush honeysuckle) S
Sow seeds in cold frame in autumn. Hardwood cuttings in cold frame in autumn/winter. Suckers – remove and replant in spring.
Dipelta S
Sow seeds outdoors in spring. Semi-ripe cuttings at 16°C (60°F) in late summer. Hardwood cuttings in cold frame in autumn.
Disanthus S
Semi-ripe cuttings at 18°C (65°F) in summer. Simple layering in summer.
Distylium T/S
Semi-ripe cuttings at 21°C (70°F) in summer. Simple layering in summer.
Drimys T/S
Sow seeds outdoors in autumn. Semi-ripe heel cuttings in cold frame in summer. Simple layering in summer.
Edgeworthia (paper bush) S
Sow seeds in cold frame in autumn. Semi-ripe cuttings at 16°C (60°F) in summer.
Eleagnus S
Sow seeds outdoors in autumn. Semi-ripe cuttings at 21°C (70°F) in autumn.
Embothrium (Chilean fire bush) T/S
Sow seeds at 16°C (60°F) in spring. Cuttings at 18°C (65°F) in summer. Root cuttings at 18°C (65°F) in winter. Suckers – remove and replant in spring.
Enkianthus S
Sow seeds at 18°C (65°F) in spring. Semi-ripe cuttings at 18°C (65°F) in autumn. Simple layering in summer.
Erica (heather) S
Sow seeds in cold frame in autumn. Semi-ripe heel cuttings in cold frame in summer. Mound layering in late spring.
Escallonia S
Sow seeds at 16°C (60°F) in spring. Semi-ripe heel cuttings in cold frame in summer. Hardwood cuttings in cold frame in autumn.
Eucalyptus (gum tree) T
Sow seeds at 16°C (60°F in early spring.
Eucryphia T/S
Sow seeds at 16°C (60°F) in spring. Semi-ripe heel cuttings at 16°C (60°F) in summer. Simple layering in summer.
Euonymus T/S
Sow seeds outdoors in spring. Semi-ripe heel cuttings in cold frame in summer/autumn. Simple layering in summer.
Eurya S
Sow seeds at 16°C (60°F) in autumn. Semi-ripe heel cuttings at 18°C (65°F) in summer.
Exochorda (pearlbush) S
Sow seeds in cold frame in autumn. Semi-ripe cuttings at 18°C (65°F) in spring. Simple layering in summer.
Fagus (beech) T
Sow seeds outdoors in autumn.
Fatsia (Japanese aralia) S
Sow seeds at 18°C (65°F) in autumn. Semi-ripe cuttings at 16°C (60°F) in summer. Suckers – remove and replant in spring.
Forsythia (golden bells) S
Semi-ripe cuttings at 16°C (60°F) in summer. Hardwood cuttings in cold frame in autumn. Simple layering in summer.
Fothergilla S
Sow seeds at 16°C (60°F) in spring. Semi-ripe cuttings at 21°C (70°F) in summer. Simple layering in summer.

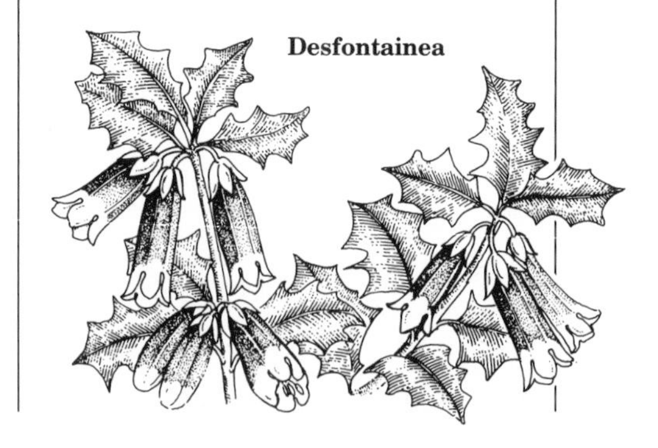
Desfontainea

Franklinia (Franklin tree) T/S
Sow seeds in cold frame in spring. Softwood cuttings at 16°C (60°F) in spring. Hardwood cuttings in cold frame in autumn.
Fraxinus (ash) T
Sow seeds outdoors in autumn.
Fremontodendron (flannel bush) S
Sow seeds at 16°C (60°F) in autumn. Softwood cuttings at 18°C (65°F) in spring. Semi-ripe cuttings in cold frame in autumn.
Fuchsia S
Sow seeds at 16°C (60°F) in spring. Softwood cuttings at 16°C (60°F) in spring. Semi-ripe cuttings in cold frame in summer.
Garrya (silk-tassel bush) S
Semi-ripe cuttings at 18°C (65°F) in summer. Hardwood cuttings at 18°C (65°F) in winter. Simple layering in summer.
Gaultheria S
Sow seeds in cold frame in spring. Semi-ripe cuttings at 16°C (60°F) in summer. Suckers – remove and replant in autumn.
Genista (broom) S
Sow seeds at 16°C (60°F) in spring. Semi-ripe cuttings in cold frame in autumn.
Ginkgo (maidenhair tree) T
Sow seeds in cold frame in autumn. Semi-ripe cuttings in cold frame in summer. Hardwood cuttings in cold frame in winter.
Gleditsia (locust) T
Sow seeds at 16°C (60°F) in autumn.
Griselinia S
Sow seeds at 16°C (60°F) in spring. Semi-ripe cuttings in cold frame in autumn.
Halesia (snowdrop tree) T/S
Sow seeds at 18°C (65°F) in autumn, chill after three months, Softwood cuttings at 18°C (65°F) in spring. Simple layering in summer.

Hamamelis (witch hazel) T/S
Sow seeds in cold frame in autumn. Softwood cuttings at 21°C (70°F) in spring. Simple layering in summer.
Hebe (shrubby veronica) S
Sow seeds in cold frame in autumn. Softwood cuttings at 16°C (60°F) in spring. Semi-ripe cuttings in cold frame in summer.
Hedera (ivy) Cl
Semi-ripe cuttings at 16°C (60°F) in summer. Leaf bud cuttings at 16°C (60°F) in summer. Serpentine layering in summer.
Helianthemum (rock rose) S
Sow seeds at 16°C (60°F) in spring. Semi-ripe heel cuttings at 16°C (60°F) in summer.
Hibiscus (rose mallow) S
Sow seeds in cold frame in spring. Semi-ripe heel cuttings at 18°C (65°F) in summer. Simple layering in summer.
Hippophae (sea buckthorn) S
Sow seeds outdoors in autumn. Hardwood cuttings in cold frame in autumn. Lift suckers and replant in spring. Simple layering in summer.
Hoheria (lacebark) T/S
Sow seeds in cold frame in autumn. Semi-ripe cuttings at 18°C (65°F) in summer. Simple layering in summer.
Hydrangea S/Cl
Sow seeds at 16°C (60°F) in spring. Softwood cuttings at 16°C (60°F) in summer. Semi-ripe cuttings at 16°C (60°F) in late summer. Serpentine layer climbers in summer.
Hypericum (St. John's wort) S
Sow seeds at 16°C (60°F) in spring. Semi-ripe cuttings in cold frame in late summer.
Ilex (holly) T/S
Sow seeds outdoors in autumn/spring. Semi-ripe cuttings at 18°C (65°F) in autumn. Simple layering in summer.

Itea T/S
Semi-ripe cuttings at 18°C (65°F) in summer. Simple layering in summer.
Jasminum (jasmine) S/Cl
Sow seeds in cold frame in autumn. Semi-ripe cuttings at 16°C (60°F) in summer. Hardwood cuttings in cold frame in autumn. Serpentine layering climbers in summer.
Juglans (walnut) T
Sow seeds outdoors in autumn.
Juniperus (juniper) C
Sow seeds outdoors in autumn. Semi-ripe heel cuttings in cold frame in late spring. Simple layering in summer.
Kalmia (calico bush) S
Sow seeds at 16°C (60°F) in spring. Semi-ripe cuttings at 16°C (60°F) in summer. Simple layering in summer.
Kerria (Jew's mallow) S
Sow seeds in cold frame in autumn. Semi-ripe cuttings in cold frame in summer. Hardwood cuttings outdoors in autumn. Simple layering in summer.
Koelreuteria (golden-rain tree) T
Sow seeds outdoors in autumn. Root cuttings at 16°C (60°F) in winter.
Kolkwitzia (beauty bush) S
Softwood cuttings at 18°C (65°F) in spring. Semi-ripe cuttings in cold frame in summer.
Laburnum (golden chain) T
Sow seeds outdoors in spring. Hardwood cuttings outdoors in autumn.
Larix (larch) C
Sow seeds outdoors in spring.
Laurus (sweet bay) T
Sow seeds outdoors in spring. Semi-ripe cuttings in cold frame in autumn.
Lavendula (lavender) S
Sow seeds at 16°C (60°F) in spring. Semi-ripe heel cuttings in cold frame in autumn.

Leptospermum (tea tree) T/S
Sow seeds at 18°C (65°F) in spring. Semi-ripe heel cuttings at 16°C (60°F) in summer.
Leucothoe S
Sow seeds at 16°C (60°F) in spring. Semi-ripe cuttings at 18°C (65°F) in summer. Simple layering in summer.
Leycesteria (Himalayan honeysuckle) S
Sow seeds in cold frame in autumn. Semi-ripe cuttings in cold frame in summer. Hardwood cuttings in cold frame in late autumn.
Ligustrum (privet) S
Sow seeds outdoors in autumn. Semi-ripe cuttings in cold frame in summer. Hardwood cuttings outdoors in autumn. Simple layering in summer.
Lippia (lemon-scented verbena) S
Softwood cuttings at 18°C (65°F) in summer.
Liriodendron (tulip tree) T
Sow seeds outdoors in autumn. Air layer in summer.
Lithospermum (gromwell) S
Sow seeds in cold frame in spring. Semi-ripe heel cuttings in cold frame in summer.
Lonicera (honeysuckle) S/Cl
Sow seeds outdoors in autumn. Semi-ripe cuttings at 16°C (60°F) in summer. Hardwood cuttings of shrubs in cold frame in autumn. Simple layering of shrubs in summer. Serpentine layering of climbers in summer.
Magnolia T/S
Sow seeds in cold frame in autumn. Simple layering in summer. Air layering in summer.
Mahonia (Oregon grape) S
Sow seeds in cold frame in autumn. Leaf bud cuttings at 18°C (60°F) in autumn.
Menziesia S
Sow seeds at 13°C (55°F) in autumn. Semi-ripe heel cuttings at 16°C (60°F) in summer. Simple layering in summer.
Mespilus (medlar) T
Sow seeds outdoors in spring. Simple or air layering in summer.
Metasequoia (dawn redwood) C
Sow seeds in cold frame in spring. Hardwood cuttings in cold frame in autumn.
Morus (mulberry) T
Hardwood cuttings outdoors in autumn. Simple layering in summer.
Myrtus (myrtle) S
Sow seeds at 16°C (60°F) in spring. Semi-ripe heel cuttings at 18°C (65°F) in summer.
Nandina (heavenly bamboo) S
Sow seeds in cold frame in autumn. Semi-ripe heel cuttings in cold frame in summer.
Nyssa (tupelo tree) T
Sow seeds in cold frame in autumn. Simple or air layering in summer.
Olearia (daisy bush) S
Semi-ripe cuttings in cold frame in summer.
Osmanthus S
Semi-ripe cuttings at 18°C (65°F) in autumn. Simple layering in summer.
Paeonia (peony) S
Sow seeds in cold frame in autumn. Simple layering in spring.
Parahebe S
Softwood cuttings at 16°C (60°F) in spring. Semi-ripe cuttings in cold frame in summer.
Parrotia (iron tree) T
Sow seeds in cold frame in autumn. Simple layering in summer.
Parthenocissus Cl
Sow seeds outdoors in autumn. Softwood cuttings at 18°C (65°F) in spring. Hardwood cuttings at 18°C (65°F) in autumn. Serpentine layering in summer.
Passiflora (passion flower) Cl
Sow seeds at 18°C (65°F) in spring. Leaf bud cuttings 18°C (65°F) in summer. Serpentine layering in summer. Suckers – remove and replant in spring.
Pernettya (prickly heath) S
Sow seeds in cold frame in autumn. Semi-ripe cuttings at 16°C (60°F) in summer.
Philadelphus (mock orange) S
Sow seeds in cold frame in autumn. Softwood cuttings at 16°C (60°F) in spring. Semi-ripe cuttings in cold frame in summer. Hardwood cuttings in cold frame in autumn.
Photinia T/S
Sow seeds in cold frame in autumn. Semi-ripe cuttings at 16°C (60°F) in summer. Simple layering in summer.
Picea (spruce) C
Sow seeds outdoors in spring. Semi-ripe cuttings at 21°C (70°F) in summer.
Pieris T/S
Sow seeds in cold frame in spring. Semi-ripe cuttings at 18°C (65°F) in summer. Simple or air layering in summer.
Pileostegia Cl
Semi-ripe cuttings at 16°C (60°F) in summer. Simple or serpentine layering in summer.
Pinus (Pine) C
Sow seeds outdoors in autumn.
Pipthanthus S
Sow seeds at 16°C (60°F) in autumn/spring.
Pittisporum T/S
Sow seeds in cold frame in autumn. Semi-ripe cuttings at 18°C (65°F) in summer.
Polygonum (Russian vine) Cl
Hardwood cuttings at 16°C (60°F) in late autumn.

Populus (poplar) T
Hardwood cuttings outdoors in autumn. Suckers – remove and replant in spring.

Potentilla S
Sow seeds in cold frame in autumn. Semi-ripe cuttings in cold frame in autumn.

Prunus (cherry/peach, etc.) T/S
Sow seeds outdoors in spring.

Pyracantha (firethorn) S
Sow seeds outdoors in autumn. Semi-ripe cuttings at 18°C (65°F) in summer.

Pyrus (pear) T
Sow seeds outdoors in autumn.

Quercus (oak) T
Sow seeds outdoors in autumn.

Rhamnus (buckthorn) T/S
Sow seeds outdoors in autumn. Semi-ripe cuttings at 16°C (60°F) in summer.

Rhododendron T/S
Sow seeds at 16°C (60°F) in spring. Semi-ripe cuttings at 21°C (70°F) in autumn. Simple layering in summer.

Rhus (sumach) T/S
Root cuttings in cold frame in winter. Suckers – remove and replant in spring.

Ribes (flowering currant) S
Hardwood cuttings outdoors in autumn.

Robinia (false acacia) T/S
Sow seeds outdoors in spring. Root cuttings in cold frame in winter. Suckers – remove and replant in spring.

◀ Sow seeds of pyracantha in autumn and subject them to the cold by leaving the container outdoors throughout the winter.

Rosa (rose) S/Cl
Sow seeds outdoors in autumn/spring. Hardwood cuttings outdoors in autumn.
Rubus (bramble) S
Root cuttings in cold frame in winter. Simple layering in summer. Divide in spring.
Ruscus (butcher's broom) S
Sow seeds in cold frame in autumn. Divide in spring.
Salix (willow) T/S
Hardwood cuttings outdoors in autumn.
Sambucus (elder) S
Sow seeds outdoors in spring. Semi-ripe cuttings at 16°C (60°F) in summer. Hardwood cuttings in cold frame in autumn.
Santolina (cotton lavender) S
Semi-ripe cuttings in cold frame in autumn. Hardwood cuttings outdoors in late autumn.
Sarcococca (sweet box) S
Sow seeds outdoors in spring. Semi-ripe cuttings in cold frame in autumn. Divide in spring.
Schizophragma Cl
Sow seeds at 18°C (65°F) in spring. Semi-ripe cuttings at 16°C (60°F) in summer. Simple or serpentine layering in summer.
Senecio S
Sow seeds at 16°C (60°F) in spring. Semi-ripe cuttings in cold frame in autumn.
Skimmia S
Sow seeds in cold frame in autumn. Semi-ripe cuttings in cold frame in autumn. Alternatively, simple layering in spring.
Sophora T/S
Sow seeds at 18°C (65°F) in early spring.
Sorbaria S
Semi-ripe heel cuttings in cold frame in summer. Hardwood cuttings in cold frame in autumn. Root cuttings in cold frame in winter. Suckers – remove and replant in autumn.
Sorbus (mountain ash) T
Sow seeds outdoors in autumn.
Spiraea S
Semi-ripe cuttings at 16°C (60°F) in summer. Hardwood cuttings in cold frame in autumn. Suckers – remove and replant in spring.
Stephanandra S
Semi-ripe cuttings in cold frame in summer. Hardwood cuttings outdoors in autumn.
Stewartia T/S
Sow seeds in cold frame in autumn. Simple or air layering in summer.
Styrax (snowbell) T/S
Sow seeds at 18°C (65°F) in spring. Semi-ripe cuttings at 16°C (60°F) in summer. Simple or air layering in summer.
Symphoricarpos (snowberry) S
Sow seeds outdoors in spring. Hardwood cuttings outdoors in autumn. Suckers – remove and replant in spring. Divide in spring.
Syringa (lilac) S
Sow seeds outdoors in autumn. Semi-ripe heel cuttings at 16°C (60°F) in summer. Root cuttings in cold frame in winter. Simple layering in summer. Suckers – remove and replant in spring.
Tamarix T/S
Sow seeds in cold frame in autumn. Hardwood cuttings outdoors in summer.
Taxus (yew) C
Sow seeds outdoors in autumn. Semi-ripe cuttings at 16°C (60°F) in autumn.
Thuja C
Sow seeds outdoors in spring. Semi-ripe cuttings in cold frame in autumn.
Tilia (lime) T
Sow seeds outdoors in autumn. Simple or air layering in summer.
Tsuga (hemlock) C
Sow seeds outdoors in autumn. Semi-ripe cuttings in cold frame in summer.
Ulex (gorse) S
Sow seeds in cold frame in spring. Softwood cuttings in cold frame in summer. Semi-ripe cuttings in cold frame in autumn.
Ulmus (elm) T
Sow seeds when ripe outdoors. Hardwood cuttings in cold frame in autumn. Suckers – remove and replant in spring. Simple or air layering in summer.
Vaccinium (blueberry) S
Sow seeds in cold frame in autumn. Semi-ripe cuttings in cold frame in summer. Simple layering in summer. Divide in spring.
Viburnum S
Sow seeds in cold frame in autumn. Semi-ripe cuttings in cold frame in summer. Hardwood cuttings in cold frame in autumn. Simple layering in summer.
Vinca (periwinkle) S
Semi-ripe cuttings in cold frame in summer. Serpentine layering in summer. Divide in spring.
Vitis (vines) Cl
Sow seeds in cold frame in autumn. Hardwood cuttings in cold frame in autumn. Serpentine layering in summer.
Weigela S
Softwood cuttings in cold frame in summer. Semi-ripe cuttings in cold frame in late summer. Hardwood cuttings in cold frame in autumn.
Wisteria Cl
Softwood cuttings at 21°C (70°F) in summer. Serpentine or simple layering in summer.
Yucca T/S
Sow seeds at 21°C (70°F) in spring. Suckers – remove and replant in spring.

· 11 ·

Herbaceous Perennials, Alpines and Water Plants

The most common herbaceous perennials, alpines and water plants have been assembled here, in an A–Z format, by the Latin generic name, for at-a-glance reference on the best methods of propagation. All of the techniques referred to in the lists are explained fully in the earlier chapters.

Acaena A
Sow in cold frame early winter. Divide in spring.
Acanthus (bear's breeches) P
Sow in cold frame early spring. Take root cuttings in cold frame early winter. Divide in spring.
Achillea P/A
Sow in cold frame mid-late spring. Take basal cuttings 16°C (60°F) mid-spring. Divide in spring.
Aconitum (monk's hood) P
Sow in cold frame early to mid-spring. Divide in spring.
Acorus (sweet flag) W
Divide late spring/early summer.
Adonis P
Sow in cold frame early spring. Divide in spring.
Aegopodium (ground elder) P
Divide early/mid spring. Take root cuttings early winter.

KEY: A = Alpine
P = Perennial
W = Water plant

Aethionema (stone cress) A
Sow in cold frame early winter. Softwood cuttings at 16°C (60°F) in summer.
Agapanthus (African lily) P
Sow seeds at 16°C (60°F) mid-spring. Divide in spring.
Ajuga (bugle) P
Divide in spring.
Alchemilla (lady's mantle) P
Sow outdoors or in cold frame in spring. Divide in spring.
Alisma (water plantain) W
Sow seeds at 16°C (60°F) in spring. Divide in spring.
Alonsoa (mask flower) P
Sow seeds at 16°C (60°F) in early spring.
Alstroemeria (Peruvian lily) P
Sow seeds at 18°C (65°F) in mid-spring. Divide in spring.
Anacyclus (Mount Atlas daisy) P
Sow seeds at 10°C (50°F) autumn/early spring. Take basal cuttings at 16°C (60°F) in spring.
Anagallis (pimpernel) P/A
Sow seeds st 16°C (60°F) in spring. Divide in spring.

Anaphalis (pearly everlasting) P
Sow seeds or take basal cuttings in cold frame in spring. Divide in spring.
Anchusa (alkanet) P
Sow seeds in cold frame early spring. Root cuttings in cold frame early winter.
Androsace (rock jessamine) A
Sow seeds when ripe outdoors or in cold frame. Divide in spring.
Anemone (wind flower) P
Sow ripe seeds outdoors in autumn. Take root cuttings in cold frame early winter. Divide in spring.
Anthemis (chamomile) P
Sow seeds outdoors late spring. Take cuttings in cold frame in spring. Divide in spring.
Anthericum (St Bernard's lily) P
Sow seeds in cold frame early spring. Divide in early spring.
Aponogeton (water hawthorn) W
Divide in spring.
Aquilegia (columbine) P
Sow seeds in cold frame or outdoors in spring.

► Roots of ***Nymphaea*** **(water lilies) are best divided in spring.**

◄ **Gather the seeds of helleborus when ripe and sow them in the cold frame.**

▼ **Left: Cut back aubrieta after flowering to produce young shoots which can be used as cuttings in later summer.**

▼ **Right: Erodium can be multiplied by taking cuttings in summer.**

Arabis (rock cress) A
Sow seeds in cold frame in spring. Semi-ripe cuttings in cold frame in summer. Divide in spring.
Arenaria (sandwort) A
Sow seeds in cold frame early winter. Basal cuttings in cold frame in summer. Divide in spring.
Arisaema P
Sow seeds at 16°C (60°F) in spring. Remove and replant offsets in spring.
Arisarum (mouse plant) P
Divide early to mid spring.
Armeria (thrift) A
Sow seeds in cold frame in early winter. Basal cuttings in cold frame in summer. Divide in spring.
Arnebia (prophet flower) P
Sow seeds at 16°C (60°F) in spring. Root cuttings at 16°C (60°F) midwinter.
Artemisia (wormwood) P
Divide in spring.
Aruncus (goat's beard) P
Sow seeds in cold frame or outdoors in spring. Divide in spring.
Arundinaria (bamboo) P
Divide in spring
Asclepias (milkweed) P
Sow seeds at 24°C (75°F) mid-spring. Divide in spring.
Asperula (woodruff) P/A
Sow seeds in cold frame or divide in spring.
Asphodeline (asphodel) P
Sow seeds in cold frame early spring. Divide in spring.
Aster (Michaelmas daisy) P
Take rooted offsets in spring.
Astilbe (false goat's beard) P
Sow seeds at 16°C (60°F) in spring. Divide in spring.
Astrantia (masterwort) P
Sow seeds in cold frame in autumn. Divide in spring.
Aubrieta A
Sow seeds in cold frame in autumn or at 16°C (60°F) in spring. Cuttings in cold frame late/summer/early autumn. Divide in autumn.
Azolla (fairy moss) W
Divide in spring.
Baptisia (false indigo) P
Sow seeds in cold frame in spring. Divide in spring.
Belamcanda (leopard flower) P
Sow seeds at 21°C (70°F) in spring. Divide in spring.
Bergenia (elephant's ears) P
Sow seeds at 18°C (60°F) in spring. Root cuttings at 21°C (70°F) in winter. Divide in spring.
Brunnera P
Sow seeds in cold frame late spring. Root cuttings in cold frame early winter. Divide in spring.
Calamintha (calamint) P
Sow seeds in cold frame or outdoors in spring. Cuttings at 16°C (60°F) in late spring. Divide in spring.
Calla (bog or water arum) W
Divide in spring.
Callitriche (water starwort) W
Soft cuttings in spring.
Caltha (marsh marigold) W
Sow seeds when ripe or in spring in cold frame. Divide in spring.
Campanula (bellflower) P/A
Sow seeds in cold frame or outdoors in late spring. Divide in spring.
Catananche (Cupid's dart) P
Sow seeds at 16°C (60°F) in early spring. Root cuttings in cold frame early winter.
Centranthus (valerian) P
Sow seeds in cold frame or outdoors in late spring. Softwood cuttings at 16°C (60°F) in late spring.
Cerastium (snow in summer) A
Sow seeds in cold frame early winter. Cuttings in cold frame spring or summer. Divide in spring.
Cerastostigma (leadwort) P
Divide in spring.
Chelone (turtlehead) P
Sow seeds at 16°C (60°F) in early spring. Basal cuttings in cold frame in spring. Divide in mid spring.
Chrysanthemum P/A
Divide or take basal cuttings in spring.
Cimicifuga (bugbane) P
Sow seeds when ripe in cold frame. Divide in spring.
Cirsium (thistle) P
Sow seeds in cold frame or outdoors in spring. Divide in spring.
Clematis P
Basal cuttings in cold frame in spring. Divide in spring.
Clintonia P
Sow seeds outdoors in late spring. Divide in spring.
Codonopsis (bonnet bellflower) P
Sow seeds in cold frame in spring. Basal cuttings in cold frame in spring.
Convallaria (lily of the valley) P
Sow seeds when ripe in cold frame. Divide in spring.
Cortaderia (pampas grass) P
Divide in spring
Cortusa P
Sow seeds when ripe in cold frame. Divide in spring.
Corydalis P/A
Sow seeds when ripe in cold frame. Divide in spring.
Cotula A
Sow seeds in cold frame in early winter. Divide in mid spring.
Crassula A
Cuttings at 16°C (60°F) in summer. Divide in spring.
Cyananthus A
Sow seeds in cold frame in early winter. Soft basal cuttings at 16°C (60°F) in early summer.
Cynoglossum (hound's tongue) P
Sow seeds outdoors in late spring. Divide in spring.

Delphinium P
Sow seeds at 13°C (55°F) in spring. Basal cuttings at 16°C (60°F) in spring. Divide in spring.
Dentaria (toothwort) P
Sow seeds in cold frame in spring. Divide in spring.
Dianthus (carnation/pink) P/A
Sow seeds at 16°C (60°F) in spring. Semi ripe cuttings in cold frame in summer. Layer in summer.
Diascia P
Sow seeds at 16°C (60°F) in early spring. Cuttings in cold frame in spring.
Dicentra (bleeding heart) P
Sow seeds at 16°C (60°F) in early spring. Root cuttings in cold frame in winter. Divide in spring.
Dictamnus (burning bush) P
Sow seeds when ripe outdoors. Divide in spring.
Dionysia A
Sow seeds when ripe in cold frame. Remove and replant offsets in summer.
Dodecatheon (shooting stars) P
Sow seeds when ripe in cold frame. Divide in spring.
Doronicum (leopard's bane) P
Sow seeds outdoors in spring. Divide after flowering.
Douglasia A
Sow seeds when ripe in cold frame. Cuttings in cold frame in summer.
Draba (whitlow grass) A
Sow seeds in cold frame in early winter. Cuttings/rosettes in cold frame in summer. Divide after flowering.
Dryas (mountain avens) A
Sow seeds when ripe in cold frame. Heel cuttings in cold frame in summer. Divide in spring.
Echinacea (purple cone flower) P
Sow seeds in cold frame or outdoors in spring. Root cuttings in cold frame in winter. Divide in spring.

Echinops (globe thistle) P
Sow seeds in cold frame or outdoors in spring. Root cuttings in cold frame in winter. Divide in spring.
Epimedium (barrenwort) P
Sow seeds when ripe in cold frame. Divide after flowering.
Erigeron (flea bane) P
Sow seeds in cold frame or outdoors in spring. Divide in spring.
Erinus (fairy foxglove) A
Sow seeds in cold frame or outdoors in spring. Divide in spring.
Erodium (stork's bill) A
Sow seeds in cold frame in early winter. Cuttings at 16°C (60°F) in summer. Root cuttings in cold frame in late winter. Divide in spring.
Eryngium (sea holly) P
Sow seeds in cold frame or outdoors in spring. Root cuttings in cold frame in winter. Divide in spring.
Erysimum P
Sow seeds in cold frame or outdoors in spring. Heel cuttings in cold frame in summer.
Euphorbia (spurge) P
Sow seeds in cold frame or outdoors in late spring. Divide in spring.
Filipendula (meadowsweet) P
Sow seeds when ripe in cold frame. Divide in spring.
Fragaria (strawberry plant) P
Sow seeds at 16°C (60°F) in spring. Layer runners in summer. Divide in spring.
Francoa P
Sow seeds in cold frame in spring. Divide in spring.
Frankenia (sea heath) P
Softwood cuttings at 16°C (60°F) in late spring. Divide in spring.
Galega (goat's rue) P
Sow seeds outdoors in late spring. Basal cuttings at 13°C (55°F) in spring. Divide in spring.
Gaura P
Sow seeds at 16°C (60°F) in spring.

Gentiana (gentian) P/A
Sow seeds when ripe in cold frame or outdoors. Basal cuttings at 16°C (60°F) in spring. Divide in spring.
Geranium (crane's bill) P/A
Sow seeds in cold frame in autumn or spring. Root cuttings in cold frame in winter. Divide in spring.
Geum (avens) P
Sow seeds when ripe in cold frame. Divide in spring.
Glaucidium P
Sow seeds in cold frame in spring. Divide in spring.
Glechoma (ground ivy) P
Softwood cuttings in cold frame spring/early summer. Divide in spring.
Gunnera P
Sow seeds at 16°C (60°F) in spring. Divide in spring.
Gypsophila (chalk plant) P/A
Sow seeds in cold frame in spring. Basal cuttings in cold frame in spring. Divide alpines in spring.
Helenium (sneezeweed) P
Sow seeds outdoors in spring. Divide in spring.
Helianthus (sunflower) P
Sow seeds outdoors in late spring. Divide in spring.
Helichrysum P/A
Sow seeds outdoors in late spring. Semi-ripe cuttings in cold frame in summer. Divide in spring.

Echinacea

Heliopsis (oxeye) P
Sow seeds outdoors in spring. Basal cuttings at 16°C (60°F) in spring. Divide in spring.
Helleborus (lenten rose/Christmas rose) P
Sow seeds when ripe in cold frame. Divide after flowering.
Hemerocallis (day lily) P
Sow seeds in cold frame or outdoors in late spring. Divide in spring.
Hepatica (liverleaf) P
Sow seeds in cold frame or outdoors in spring. Divide after flowering.
Hesperis (sweet rocket) P
Sow seeds outdoors in spring. Divide in spring.
Heuchera (alum root) P
Sow seeds in cold frame in spring. Divide in spring.
Hosta (plantain lily) P
Sow seeds in cold frame in spring. Divide in spring.
Hottonia (water violet) W
Divide in spring.
Houstonia (bluets) P/A
Divide in spring.
Houttuynia P
Sow seeds in cold frame in spring. Divide in spring.
Hutchinsia A
Sow seeds in cold frame in early winter. Divide in spring.
Hydrocharia (frogbit) W
Detach rooted runners in spring.
Iberis (candytuft) P/A
Sow seeds at 16°C (60°F) in early spring. Cuttings in cold frame in summer.
Incarvillea P
Sow seeds at 16°C (60°F) in spring. Divide in spring.
Inula P
Sow seeds outdoors in late spring. Divide in spring.
Jeffersonia A
Sow seeds when ripe in cold frame. Divide in spring.

Knautia P
Sow seeds outdoors in late spring. Divide in spring.
Kniphofia (red-hot poker) P
Sow seeds in cold frame or outdoors in late spring. Divide in spring.
Lamium (dead nettle) P
Sow seeds outdoors in late spring. Divide in spring.
Leontopodium (edelweiss) A
Sow seeds in cold frame in late autumn. Divide in spring.
Lewisia A
Sow seeds when ripe in cold frame. Remove and replant offsets in early summer. Divide in spring.
Liatris (gayfeather) P
Sow seeds in cold frame in early spring. Divide in spring.
Libertia P
Sow seeds when ripe in cold frame. Divide in spring.
Ligularia P
Sow seeds outdoors in late spring. Divide in spring.
Limonium (sea lavender) P
Sow seeds at 16°C (60°F) in spring. Root cuttings in cold frame in winter. Divide in spring.
Linaria (toadflax) P
Sow seeds in cold frame in spring. Softwood cuttings at 16°C (60°F) in late spring. Divide in spring.
Linum (flax) P/A
Sow seeds in cold frame in spring. Cuttings at 16°C (60°F) in spring.
Liriope (lilyturf) P
Sow seeds when ripe in cold frame. Divide in spring.
Lobelia P
Sow seeds at 16°C (60°F) in spring. Divide in spring.
Lupin P
Sow seeds at 16°C (60°F) in spring. Basal cuttings in cold frame in spring.
Luzula (woodrush) P
Divide in spring.

Lychnis (campion) P
Sow seeds outdoors in late spring. Basal cuttings in cold frame in spring. Divide in spring.
Lysichiton (skunk cabbage) P
Sow seeds when ripe in cold frame. Divide after flowering.
Lysimachia (loosestrife) P
Sow seeds outdoors in late spring. Basal cuttings in cold frame in spring. Divide in spring.
Lythrum P
Sow seeds outdoors in late spring. Basal cuttings in cold frame in spring. Divide in spring.
Malva (mallow) P
Sow seeds at 16°C (60°F) in spring. Basal cuttings in cold frame in spring.
Mazus A
Sow seeds when ripe in cold frame. Divide in spring.
Meconopsis (blue and Welsh poppy) P
Sow seeds when ripe in cold frame. Divide in spring.
Melissa (balm) P
Sow seeds outdoors in spring. Divide in spring.
Mertensia (smooth lungwort) P
Sow seeds when ripe in cold frame. Divide in spring.
Mimulus (monkey flower) P
Sow seeds at 16°C (60°F) in early spring. Softwood cuttings 16°C (60°F) in spring. Divide in spring.
Miscanthus P
Divide in spring.
Mitella (mitrewort) P
Sow seeds at 16°C (60°F) in spring. Divide in spring.
Monarda (bergamot) P/A
Sow seeds at 16°C (60°F) in spring. Divide in spring.

► Create a colourful herbaceous border by raising plants from seed, cuttings or by division.

Montia P/A
Sow seeds when ripe in cold frame. Divide in spring.
Morina P
Sow seeds in cold frame in spring. Divide in spring.
Myriophyllum (water milfoil) W
Soft cuttings in late spring. Divide in spring.
Nepeta (catmint) P
Sow seeds at 16°C (60°F) in spring. Basal cuttings at 16°C (60°F) in late spring. Divide in spring.
Nierembergia (cup flower) P
Sow seeds at 13°C (55°F) in spring. Cuttings at 16°C (60°F) in late spring. Divide in spring.
Nymphaea (water lily) W
Sow seeds when ripe at 16°C (60°F). Divide in mid/late spring.
Oenothera (evening primrose) P
Sow seeds at 16°C (60°F) in spring. Softwood cuttings in cold frame in late spring. Divide in spring.
Omphalodes (navelwort) P/A
Sow seeds in cold frame in spring. Divide in spring.
Orontium (golden club) W
Sow seeds when ripe in shallow water at 16°C (60°F). Divide in spring.
Paeonia (peony) P
Sow seeds when ripe in cold frame. Divide in spring.
Peltandra (arrow arum) A
Divide in spring.
Penstemon (beard tongue) P/A
Sow seeds at 16°C (60°F), alpines in cold frame in early spring. Softwood cuttings in cold frame in spring. Semi-ripe cuttings in cold frame in late summer. Divide in spring.
Perovskia P
Sow seeds at 16°C (60°F) in early spring. Semi-ripe cuttings in cold frame in summer.
Phlomis P
Sow seeds at 16°C (60°F) in spring. Semi-ripe cuttings at 16°C (60°F) in summer.
Phlox P/A
Sow alpines in cold frame in early winter. Semi-ripe cuttings of alpines in cold frame in summer. Soft basal cuttings of perennials in cold frame in spring. Root cuttings of perennials in cold frame in winter.
Phormium (New Zealand flax) P
Sow seeds at 16°C (60°F) in spring. Divide in spring.
Physalis (Chinese lantern) P
Sow seeds in cold frame in spring. Root cuttings in cold frame in winter. Divide in spring.

Physalis

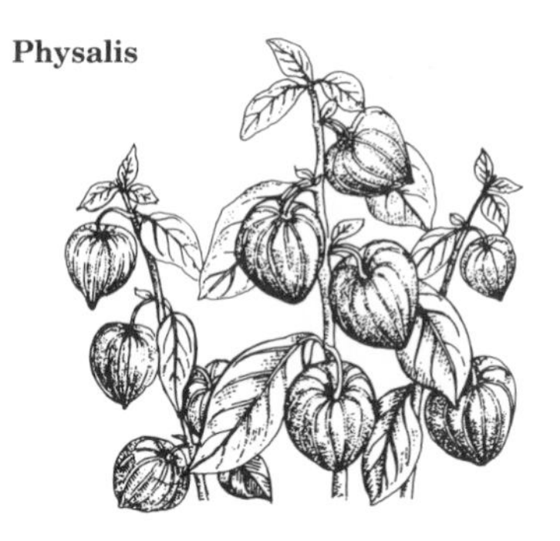

Physostegia (obedient plant) P
Sow seeds in cold frame in autumn. Basal cuttings in cold frame in spring. Divide in spring.
Phytolacca (pokeweed) P
Sow seeds outdoors in late spring. Divide in spring.
Platycodon (balloon flower) P
Sow seeds in cold frame in spring. Basal cuttings 16°C (60°F) in spring. Divide in spring.
Polemonium (Jacob's ladder) P
Sow seeds when ripe outdoors. Divide in spring.
Polygala (milk wort) A
Cuttings in cold frame in early summer. Divide in spring.
Polygonatum (Solomon's seal) P
Sow seeds when ripe in cold frame. Section rhizomes at 16°C (60°F) in spring. Divide in spring.
Polygonum (knotweed) P
Semi-ripe cuttings in cold frame in summer. Divide in spring.
Pontederia (pickerel weed) W
Divide in spring.
Potentilla (cinquefoil) P/A
Sow seeds in cold frame, alpines in autumn, perennials in spring. Cuttings of perennials in cold frame in spring. Divide both in spring.
Pratia A
Sow seeds in cold frame in spring. Layer in spring. Semi-ripe cuttings at 16°C (60°F) in summer. Divide in spring.
Primula P/A
Sow seeds when ripe in cold frame. Divide in spring.
Prunella (self heal) P
Sow seeds in cold frame or outdoors in spring. Divide in spring.
Pulmonaria (lungwort) P
Sow seeds in cold frame or outdoors in spring. Divide in spring.
Pulsatilla (pasque flower) P
Sow seeds when ripe in cold frame. Root cuttings in cold frame in winter.
Pyrethrum P
Sow seeds at 16°C (60°F) in spring. Basal cuttings at 16°C (60°F) in spring. Divide after flowering.
Ramonda (rosette mullein) A
Sow seeds in cold frame in spring. Leaf cuttings in cold frame in summer.
Ranunculus P/A
Sow seeds when ripe in cold frame in autumn. Divide in spring.
Raoulia A
Divide in summer.
Rheum (ornamental rhubarb) P
Sow seeds outdoors in spring. Divide in spring.

Rhodohypoxis A
Sow seeds in cold frame in spring. Divide in spring.
Rodgersia P
Sow seeds in cold frame in spring. Divide in spring.
Romneya (Californian tree poppy) P
Sow seeds at 16°C (60°F) in early spring. Root cuttings at 16°C (60°F) in winter. Remove suckers and replant in spring.
Roscoea P
Sow seeds when ripe in cold frame. Divide in spring.
Rudbeckia (coneflower) P
Sow seeds at 16°C (60°F) in early spring. Divide in spring.
Sagittaria (arrowhead) W
Divide in spring.
Salvia (sage) P
Sow seeds at 16°C (60°F) in spring. Cuttings at 16°C (60°F) in late spring/early summer. Divide in spring.
Sanguinaria (bloodroot) P
Sow seeds in cold frame in autumn. Divide in late spring.
Saponaria (soapwort) P
Sow seeds in cold frame in spring. Softwood cuttings in cold frame in early summer. Divide in spring.
Saxifraga (saxifrage) A
Surface sow seeds in cold frame in autumn. Cuttings/rosettes in cold frame in early summer. Divide in spring or after flowering.
Scabious (pincushion flower) P
Sow seeds in cold frame in late spring. Basal cuttings in cold frame in early spring. Divide in spring.
Scutellaria (skull cap) A
Sow seeds in cold frame in spring. Divide in summer.
Sedum (stonecrop) P/A
Sow seeds in cold frame in spring. Softwood cuttings in cold frame in early summer. Divide in spring.
Sempervivum (house leek) A
Rooted offsets at any time in cold frame or outdoors.
Shortia P
Sow seeds in cold frame in spring. Divide after flowering.
Sidalcea (Greek mallow) P
Sow seeds in cold frame in spring. Basal cuttings at 16°C (60°F) in spring. Divide in spring.
Silene (catchfly) P/A
Sow seeds in cold frame or outdoors in spring. Basal cuttings in cold frame in spring. Divide in spring.
Sisyrinchium (satin flower) P
Sow seeds in cold frame early autumn/early spring. Divide in spring.
Smilacina (false Solomon's seal) P
Sow seeds in cold frame in spring. Divide in autumn.
Soldanella A
Sow seeds when ripe in cold frame. Divide in early summer.
Solidago (golden rod) P
Sow seeds in cold frame in spring. Divide after flowering.
Stachys (lamb's tongue) P
Sow seeds in cold frame in spring. Divide in spring.
Stokesia (Stokes' aster) P
Sow seeds in cold frame in spring. Root cuttings in cold frame in early winter. Divide in spring.
Stratiotes (water soldier) W
Remove and replant offsets in late spring/early summer.
Tanacetum P
Sow seeds at 16°C (60°F) in spring. Basal cuttings at 16°C (60°F) in spring. Divide in spring.
Tellimia P
Sow seeds in cold frame in spring. Divide in spring.
Thalictrum (meadow rue) P
Sow seeds in cold frame in spring. Divide in spring.
Tiarella (foam flower) P
Sow seeds in cold frame in spring. Divide in spring.
Tolmiea (pick-a-back plant) P
Sow seeds in cold frame in spring. Divide in spring.
Tradescantia (spiderwort) P
Sow seeds in cold frame in spring. Divide in spring.
Tricyrtis (toad lily) P
Sow seeds in cold frame in spring. Divide in spring.
Trollius (globe flower) P
Sow seeds when ripe in cold frame. Divide in spring.
Tropaeolum P
Sow seeds in cold frame in spring. Basal cuttings at 16°C (60°F) in spring. Divide in spring.
Typha (reedmace) W
Divide in spring.
Utricularia (bladderwort) W
Divide in spring.
Uvularia (bellwort) P
Divide in spring.
Verbena (vervain) P
Sow seeds at 18°C (65°F) spring. Semi-ripe cuttings in cold frame in summer.
Veronica (speedwell) P/A
Sow seeds in cold frame or outdoors in spring. Basal cuttings in cold frame in spring, cuttings of alpines in cold frame in summer. Divide in spring.
Viola P/A
Sow seeds in cold frame in spring. Basal cuttings in cold frame in late summer. Divide in spring.
Waldsteinia P
Divide in spring.

Sempervivum

▲ ***Venidium fastuosum* is easily raised from seed sown in spring.**

► Sweet peas sown in winter will flower earlier than those sown in spring.

· 12 ·
Annuals and Biennials

The most common annual and biennial plants have been assembled here, in an A–Z format, by the Latin generic name, for at-a-glance reference on the best methods of propagation. All of the techniques referred to in the lists that follow are explained fully in the earlier chapters.

Adonis (pheasant's eye) HA
Sow seeds direct outdoors in spring.
Ageratum (floss flower) HHA
Sow seeds at 21°C (70°F) late winter/early spring.
Agrostemma (corn cockle) HA
Sow seed direct outdoors in spring.
Althaea (hollyhock) HP treat as HB/HHA
Sow HB in outdoor seed bed early summer, sow HHA at 13°C (55°F) in late winter/early spring.
Alyssum HA
Sow indoors at 13°C (55°F) late winter/early spring or outdoors mid to late spring.
Amaranthus (love lies bleeding) HHA
Sow at 13-16°C (55-60°F) late winter/early spring.

KEY:
HP = Hardy perennial
HHP = Half-hardy perennial
HA = Hardy annual
HHA = Half-hardy annual
HB = Hardy biennial

Ammobium (winged everlasting) HHA
Sow at 13-16°C (55-60°F) in early spring.
Anchusa HA
Sow direct outdoors in spring.
Antirrhinum (snapdragon) HP treat as HHA
Sow at 18°C (65°F) in late winter.
Arctotis (African daisy) HHA
Sow at 16–18°C (60–65°F) late winter/early spring.
Argemone (prickly poppy) HA
Sow direct outdoors in spring.
Aster HHA
Sow at 16–18°C (60–65°F) in mid-spring.
Asperula (woodruff) HA
Sow direct outdoors in spring.
Atriplex (orach) HA
Sow direct outdoors in spring.
Bartonia (blazing star) HA
Sow direct outdoors in spring.
Begonia HHP treat as HHA
Surface sow at 21–24°C (70–75°F) in late winter.
Bellis perennis (daisy) HB
Sow in outdoor seed bed in early summer.
Bidens HHP treat as HHA
Sow at 16°C (60°F) in early spring.

Brachycome (swan river daisy) HHA
Sow at 16°C (60°F) in early spring.
Brompton stock HB
Sow in outdoor seed bed in early summer.
Bupleurum (hare's ear) HA
Sow in flowering position in spring.
Calceolaria (slipper flower) HA/HHA
Surface sow HHA at 18–21°C (65–70°F) late winter/early spring and HA directly outdoors mid-spring.
Calendula (English marigold) HA
Sow in flowering position in spring.
Campanula (Canterbury bells) HB
Sow in outdoor seed bed in early summer.
Centaurea (cornflower) HA
Sow in flowering position in spring.
Cheiranthus (wallflower) HB
Sow in outdoor seed bed in early summer.
Chrysanthemum HA
Sow in flowering position in mid-spring.
Cladanthus (Palm Spring's daisy) HHA
Sow at 13–16°C (55–60°F) in early spring.

Clarkia HA
Sow in flowering position in mid-spring.
Clary (salvia horminum) HA
Sow in flowering position in mid-spring.
Cleome (spider flower) HHA
Sow at 18–21°C (65–70°F) in mid-spring.
Convolvulus (morning glory) HA
Sow in flowering position mid to late spring.
Coreopsis HP treat as HHA
Sow indoors at 13°C (55°F) in late winter.
Cosmidium HHA
Sow at 16°C (60°F) in early spring.
Cosmos HHA
Sow at 16°C (60°F) in early spring.
Crepis (hawkweed) HA
Sow indoors at 13°C (55°F) in early spring or in flowering position mid or late spring.
Delphinium ajacis (rocket larkspur) HA
Sow in flowering position in spring.
Dianthus (carnations/pinks) HHA
Sow at 16°C (60°F)in late winter/early spring.
Dianthus barbatus (sweet william) HB
Sow outdoors in seed bed in early summer.

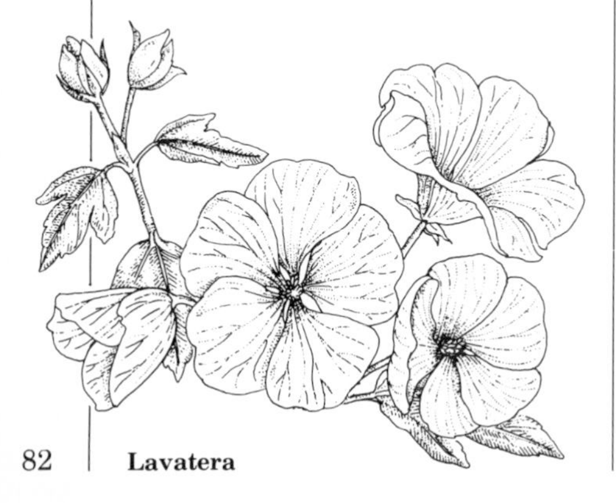
Lavatera

Digitalis (foxglove) HB
Sow in outdoor seed bed in early summer.
Dipsacus sativus (teasel) HB
Sow outdoors in seed bed in early summer.
Echium (viper's bugloss) HA
Sow in flowering position mid or late spring.
Euphorbia (spurge) HA
Sow in flowering position mid or late spring.
Eustoma (prairy gentian) HHP treat as HHA
Sow at 21°C (70°F) in late winter/early spring.
Felicia (kingfisher daisy) HHA/HA
Sow HHA at 16°C (60°F) late winter/early spring. Sow HA direct outdoors in spring.
Gaillardia (blanket flower) HHA
Sow at 16°C (60°F) in late winter/early spring.
Gazania (treasure flower) HHP treat as HHA
Sow at 16–18°C (60–65°F) late winter/early spring.
Gilia (birds eyes) HA
Sow in flowering position in spring.
Godetia HA
Sow in flowering position in spring.
Gomphrena HHA
Sow at 16–18°C (60–65°F) in early spring.
Gypsophila (baby's breath) HA
Sow in flowering position in spring.
Helianthus (sunflower) HA
Sow in flowering position in early to mid-spring.
Helichrysum (straw flower) HHA
Sow at 16°C (60°F) in late winter/early spring.
Helipterum (rhodanthe) HA
Sow in flowering position in mid or late spring.
Iberis (candytuft) HA
Sow in flowering position in spring.

Impatiens (busy lizzie) HHP treat as HHA
Surface sow at 21–24°C (70–75°F) in late winter/early spring.
Ipomoea (morning glory) HHA
Sow at 21°C (70°F) in late winter.
Kochia (burning bush) HHA
Sow at 21°C (70°F) in late winter/early spring.
Lathyrus (sweet pea) HA
Sow at 16°C (60°F) mid to late winter or outdoors in early to mid-spring.
Lavatera (mallow) HA
Sow in flowering position in early spring.
Layia (tidy tips) HA
Sow in flowering position in early spring.
Limnanthes (poached egg plant) HA
Sow in flowering position in early spring.
Limonium (statice) HHA
Sow at 18°C (65°F) in late winter/early spring.
Linanthus (mountain phlox) HA
Sow in flowering position in early spring.
Linaria (toadflax) HA
Sow in flowering position in early spring.
Linum (flax) HA
Sow in flowering position in spring.
Lobelia HHA
Surface sow at 21°C (70°F) mid-winter to early spring.
Lonas inodora HHA
Sow at 16°C (60°F) late winter to early spring.
Lunaria (honesty) HB
Sow in outdoor seed bed in early summer.
Malcolmia (Virginian stock) HA
Sow in flowering position early to mid-spring.
Malope (malva) HA
Sow in flowering position early to mid-spring.

Marigold HHA
Sow at 13-16°C (55-60°F) late winter to mid spring.
Matricaria HP treat as HHA
Sow at 13°C (55°F) in late winter to early spring.
Matthiola (stocks) HHA
Sow at 16°C (60°F) in late winter to mid-spring.
Matthiola bicornis (night-scented stock) HA
Sow in flowering position in early to mid-spring.
Mesembryanthemum (Livingstone daisy) HHA
Sow at 16°C (60°F) in early to mid-spring.
Mimulus (monkey flower) HP treat as HHA
Sow at 21°C (70°F) in late winter to early spring.
Mirabilis (marvel of Peru) HHA
Sow at 16°C (60°F) in late winter to mid spring.
Moluccella laevis (bells of Ireland) HHA
Sow and chill in salad drawer of refrigerator for 14 days, transfer to 16°C (60°F) in spring.
Myosotis (forget-me-not) HB
Sow in outdoor seed bed in early summer.
Nemesia HHA
Sow at 16°C (60°F) in late winter to early spring.
Nemophila (baby blue eyes) HA
Sow in flowering position in early to mid-spring.
Nicandra (shoo fly plant) HA
Sow in flowering position in early to mid-spring.
Nicotiana (tobacco plant) HHA
Sow at 21°C (70°F) in late winter to mid-spring.
Nierembergias (cup flower) HHP treat as HHA
Sow at 13°C (55°F) in late winter to early spring.

Nigella (love-in-a-mist) HA
Sow in flowering position late winter to mid-spring.
Nolana HHP treat as HHA
Sow at 16°C (60°F) in late winter to early spring.
Osteospermum (star of the veldt) HHA
Sow at 16°C (60°F) in late winter to early spring.
Papaver (poppy) HA
Sow in flowering position in early to mid-spring.
Papaver nudicaule (Iceland poppy) HB
Sow in outdoor seed bed in early summer.
Penstemon (beard tongue) HP treat as HHA
Sow at 16°C (60°F) in late winter/early spring.
Petunia HHA
Surface sow at 21°C (70°F) late winter to early spring.
Phacelia (Californian bluebell) HA
Sow in flowering position in mid to late spring.
Phlox drummondii HHA
Sow at 16°C (60°F) in late winter/early spring.
Portulaca (sun plant) HHA
Sow at 18°C (65°F) in late winter/early spring.
Reseda (mignonette) HA
Sow in flowering position in early to mid-spring.
Rudbeckia (cone flower) HHA
Sow at 16°C (60°F) in late winter/early spring.
Salpiglossis HHA
Sow at 16°C (60°F) in late winter/early spring.
Salvia HHP treat as HHA
Sow at 21°C (70°F) in late winter to mid-spring.
Sanvitalia (creeping zinnia) HHA
Sow at 16°C (60°F) in late winter/early spring.

Saponaria (soapwort) HA
Sow in flowering position in early to mid-spring.
Scabious (pincushion flower) HA
Sow in flowering position in early to mid-spring.
Schizanthus (butterfly flower) HHA
Sow at 16°C (60°F) in late winter/mid-spring.
Tagetes HHA
Sow at 13–16°C (55–60°F) late winter to mid-spring.
Thunbergia (black-eyed Susan) HHA
Sow at 18°C (65°F) in late winter to mid-spring.
Tithonia (Mexican sunflower) HHA
Sow at 18°C (65°F) in late winter/early spring.
Tolpis HHA
Sow at 16°C (60°F) in early to mid-spring.
Tropaeolum (nasturtium) HA
Sow in flowering position in early to mid-spring.
Ursinia HHA
Sow at 18°C (65°F) in late winter to mid-spring.
Venidium (Monarch of the Veldt) HHA
Sow at 16°C (60°F) in early to mid-spring.
Verbena HHA
Sow at 16°C (60°F) in late winter to mid-spring.
Viola x wittrodeiana (pansy) HP treat as HHA
Sow at 13°C (55°F) mid-winter to early spring. Sow winter flowering in late spring.
Viscaria (*Silene coeli-rosa*) HA
Sow in flowering position in early to mid-spring.
Zinnia HHA
Sow at 21–24°C (70–75°F) in early spring.

· 13 ·
Bulbous Plants

The most common garden bulbs have been assembled here in an A–Z format, by the Latin generic name, for at-a-glance reference on the best methods of propagation. All of the techniques referred to in the lists that follow are explained fully in the earlier chapters.

Achimenes
Sow seeds or plant tubers at 18–21°C (65–70°F) in late winter.
Acidanthera
Sow seeds at 13°C (55°F) in early spring. Plant cormlets in late winter.
Allium
Sow seeds outdoors when ripe. Divide clumps in autumn.
Amaryllis belladonna
Sow seeds at 16°C (60°F) in early spring. Lift and remove offsets in late summer.
Anemone
Sow ripe seeds outdoors in late summer. Lift and divide tubers when dormant.
Anthericum
Sow seeds in cold frame in early spring. Divide clumps in autumn/early spring.
Arum
Sow seeds outdoors in autumn. Divide tubers in early spring.
Brodiaea
Sow seeds at 16°C (60°F) in early spring. Lift and divide when dormant.
Buldocodium
Lift and divide when dormant. Plant offsets in early autumn.
Cardiocrinum
Sow seeds at 13°C (55°F) when ripe or in early spring. Lift and divide when dormant.
Chionodoxa
Sow ripe seeds in cold frame in autumn. Lift and divide when dormant.
Clivia
Remove and plant offsets at 13°C (55°F) in late winter/early spring. Sow seeds when ripe at 16°C (60°F).
Colchicum
Sow seeds outdoors or in cold frame in late summer. Lift and divide when dormant.
Crocosmia
Sow seeds in cold frame in autumn. Lift and divide clumps in autumn.
Crocus
Sow seeds in cold frame in autumn. Lift and divide clump when dormant.
Cyclamen
Sow hardy varieties in cold frame in early autumn. Sow others at 16°C (60°F) in autumn or late winter.
Dahlia
Divide dormant tubers and plant in mid-spring. Take cuttings from tubers and plant late spring.
Dierama
Sow seeds in cold frame in early spring. Lift and divide in mid autumn.
Endymion
Sow seed outdoors when ripe. Lift and divide when dormant.
Eranthus
Sow seeds in cold frame in early autumn. Divide in mid-autumn.
Eremurus
Sow seeds at 16°C (60°F) in early spring. Divide in early autumn.
Erythronium
Sow seeds in cold frame in autumn. Divide when dormant.
Eucharis
Sow seeds at 24°C (75°F) in early spring. Alternatively, remove offsets in late spring.
Eucomis
Remove and replant offsets in autumn.
Freesia
Soak seeds before sowing at 16°C (60°F) in spring. Divide when dormant.
Fritillaria
Sow seeds in cold frame when ripe. Remove and replant offsets in late summer.

Galanthus (snowdrop)
Sow seeds outdoors when ripe. Divide and replant after flowering.
Galtonia
Sow seeds in cold frame in spring. Remove and replant offsets in autumn.
Gladiolus
Lift and divide in autumn.
Gloriosa
Sow seeds or plant offsets at 21°C (70°F) in late winter/early spring.
Haemanthus
Remove offsets and plant at 16°C (60°F) in spring or autumn.
Hippeastrum
Sow seeds at 18°C (65°F) in early spring. Remove offsets when repotting.
Hyacinth
Sow seeds in cold frame when ripe. Remove and replant bulbils when dormant.
Hymenocallis
Remove offsets when repotting.
Ipheion
Lift and divide in autumn or spring.
Iris
Divide rhizomes in summer. Lift and divide bulbs when dormant.
Ixia
Sow seeds at 16°C (60°F) in early spring. Divide and replant when dormant.
Lachenalia
Remove and replant bulbils in late summer.
Leucojum
Sow seeds in cold frame in autumn. Lift and divide when dormant.
Lilium
Sow seeds in cold frame in autumn. Lift and divide when dormant.
Muscari
Sow seeds in cold frame in autumn. Lift and divide when dormant.
Narcissus
Sow seeds in cold frame in late summer. Lift and divide when dormant.
Nerine
Sow seeds in cold frame when ripe. Lift and divide when dormant.

Lilium lancifolium **(tiger lily)**

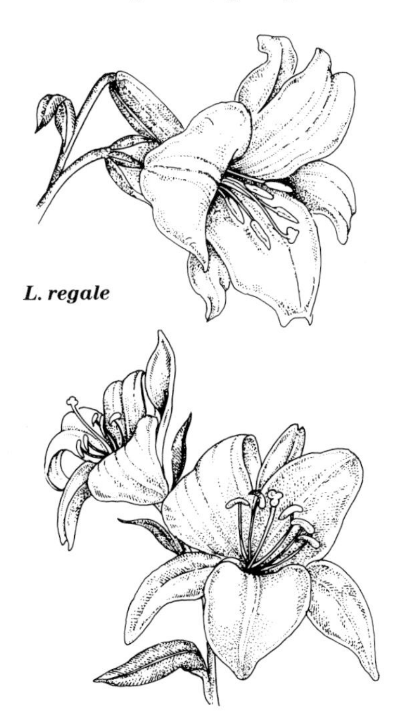

L. regale

L. candidum **'Madonna'**

Ornithogalum
Sow seeds in cold frame when ripe. Lift and divide when dormant.
Oxalis
Sow seeds at 16°C (60°F) in spring. Lift and divide when dormant.
Puschkinia
Sow seeds in cold frame in autumn. Lift and divide when dormant.
Ranunculus
Lift and divide when dormant.
Rhodohypoxis
Sow seeds in cold frame or divide in spring.
Schizostylis
Lift and divide in early spring.
Scilla
Sow seeds outdoors when ripe. Lift and divide when dormant.
Sparaxis
Sow ripe seeds at 16°C (60°F). Lift and divide in autumn.
Sprekelia
Remove offsets when repotting.
Sternbergia
Lift and divide in autumn.
Tigridia
Sow seeds at 16°C (60°F) in early spring. Lift and divide in autumn.
Trillium
Sow seeds in cold frame when ripe. Lift and divide when dormant.
Tritonia
Sow seeds at 16°C (60°F) in early spring. Divide when dormant.
Tropaeolum
Lift tubers in autumn. Divide in spring or autumn.
Tulipa (tulip)
Sow seeds when ripe in cold frame. Lift and divide when dormant.
Vallota
Sow seeds at 16°C (60°F) in early spring. Remove offsets when repotting.
Zantedeschia
Soak seeds and sow at 24°C (75°F) in early spring. Divide in spring.

· 14 ·
House and Conservatory Plants

The most common type of house and conservatory plant have been assembled here, in an A–Z format, by the Latin generic name, for at-a-glance reference on the best methods of propagation. All of the techniques referred to in the lists that follow are explained fully in the earlier chapters.

Abutilon
Sow seeds at 16°C (60°F) in early to mid-spring. Tip cuttings in spring or summer.
Acacia
Sow seeds at 18°C (65°F) in mid-spring. Semi-ripe cuttings in mid-summer.
Acalypha
Stem cuttings at 21°C (70°F) in mid-spring.
Aeschynanthus
Tip cuttings at 18°C (65°F) in late spring/early summer.
Anthurium
Divide roots in spring.
Aphelandra
Tip cuttings in late spring.
Asparagus
Sow seeds at 21°C (70°F) or divide in spring.
Aspidistra
Divide in spring.
Azalea
Heel cuttings at 16°C (60°F) in early summer.
Begonia
Surface sow seeds at 21°C (70°F) in spring. Stem or leaf cuttings or divide tubers at 18°C (65°F) in late spring/early summer.
Beloperone
Tip cuttings at 18°C (65°F) in spring.
Bougainvillea
Tip cuttings at 21°C (70°F) in spring.
Bromelliad family
Surface sow seeds or take offsets at 24°C (75°F) in spring.
Browallia
Sow seeds at 16°C (60°F) in spring.
Brunfelsia
Tip cuttings at 18°C (65°F) in spring.
Cacti
Surface sow seeds at 21°C (70°F). Remove offsets, if produced, in spring.
Caladium
Divide and repot tubers in early spring.
Calceolaria
Surface sow seeds at 18°C (65°F) in early summer.
Callistemon
Sow seeds at 18°C (65°F) in early spring. Semi-ripe heel cuttings at 18°C (65°F) in summer.
Campanula
Sow seeds at 13–16°C (55–60°F) in late winter. Divide or take tip cuttings in spring.
Capsicum
Sow seeds at 18°C (65°F) in early spring.
Catharanthus
Sow seeds at 18°C (65°F) in early spring.
Celosia
Sow seeds at 18°C (65°F) in late winter.
Cestrum
Semi-ripe cuttings at 21°C (70°F) in summer.
Chlorophytum
Divide in early spring. Root plantlets any time.
Cineraria
Sow seeds at 13°C (55°F) in late spring/early summer.
Cissus
Tip cuttings at 18°C (65°F) in summer.
Citrus
Sow seeds at 16°C (60°F) in spring or summer. Semi-ripe cuttings in summer.
Clianthus
Sow seeds at 18°C (65°F) in early spring. Heel cuttings in summer.

Coleus
Sow seeds at 18°C (65°F) in late winter/early summer. Tip cuttings at 16°C (60°F) when available.
Columnea
Take cuttings at 18°C (65°F) in spring.
Crossandra
Sow seeds at 18°C (65°F) in early spring. Softwood cuttings at 21°C (70°F) in spring.
Croton (Codiaeum)
Tip cuttings st 21°C (70°F) in spring.
Cuphea
Sow seeds at 16°C (60°F) in late winter. Tip cuttings at 18°C (65°F) in early spring.
Cyperus
Divide or place flower head upside down in water or damp compost in spring.
Cytisus
Tip cuttings at 16°C (60°F) in spring.
Datura
Sow seeds at 16°C (60°F) in early spring. Heel cuttings at 18°C (65°F) in late spring.
Dieffenbachia
Tip cuttings at 21°C (70°F) in spring. Air layer in spring or summer.
Dipladenia
Heel cuttings at 18°C (65°F) in early spring.
Dizygotheca
Sow seeds at 21°C (70°F) in late winter.
Dracaena
Take basal shoots or tip cuttings at 21°C (70°F) in early spring.
Euphorbia pulcherrima
(poinsettia)
Tip cuttings at 18°C (65°F) in late spring.
Exacum
Surface sow seeds at 18°C (65°F) in early spring.
Fatshedera
Tip cuttings at 18°C (65°F) in spring.
Fatsia
Sow seeds at 13°C (55°F) in mid-spring. Root suckers in cold frame in early spring.
Ficus
Surface sow seeds at 24°C (75°F) in spring. Root cuttings in late spring. Air layer in early summer.
Fittonia
Divide at 18–21°C (65–70°F) in spring.
Gardenia
Take heel cuttings at 18°C (65°F) in early spring.
Gloriosa
Sow seeds at 21°C (70°F) in early spring. Remove offsets in late winter, start into growth at 18°C (65°F).
Gloxinia
Surface sow at 21°C (70°F) in late winter/early spring.
Grevillea
Surface sow at 21°C (70°F) in spring. Heel cuttings at 18°C (65°F) in mid-summer.
Gynura
Tip cuttings at 18°C (65°F) in mid-spring.
Hedera (ivy)
Root cuttings at 13°C (55°F) in late spring/summer. Layer in spring.
Helxine
Detach rooted stems in spring/summer.
Heptapleurum
Stem cuttings at 18°C (65°F) in spring.
Hibiscus
Heel cuttings at 18°C (65°F) spring/early summer.
Hoya
Stem cuttings 18°C (65°F) in early summer. Layer in spring.
Hypoestes
Sow seeds at 18°C (65°F) in early spring. Cuttings at 18°C (65°F) in spring.
Iresine
Tip cuttings at 16°C (60°F) in spring.
Jasmine
Heel cuttings at 16°C (60°F) in summer.
Kalanchoe
Surface sow seeds at 21°C (70°F) in early spring. Stem cuttings at 16°C (60°F) in summer.
Lantana
Sow seeds at 16°C (60°F) in late winter. Tip cuttings at 16°C (60°F) in summer.
Maranta
Divide or take basal cuttings at 21°C (70°F) in spring/summer.
Mimosa
Sow seeds at 21°C (70°F) in early spring.
Monstera
Tip cuttings at 24°C (75°F) in early summer.
Nerium
Sow seeds at 21°C (70°F) in early spring. Semi-ripe cuttings at 16°C (60°F) in early summer.
Nertera
Divide at 16°C (60°F) in spring.
Pachystachys
Tip cuttings at 21°C (70°F) in the spring.
Palm
Sow seeds or remove offsets at 21°C (70°F) in spring.
Passiflora
Sow seeds at 18°C (65°F) in spring. Take cuttings at 16°C (60°F) in early summer.
Peperomia
Stem or leaf cuttings at 18°C (65°F) in spring/summer.
Philodendron
Sow seeds at 24°C (75°F) in early spring. Divide or take tip cuttings at 24°C (75°F) in spring.
Pilea
Take cuttings at 18°C (65°F) in late spring.

▲ **Streptocarpus can be raised by sowing the seeds or taking leaf cuttings.**

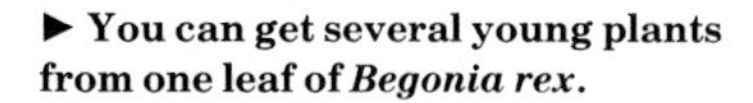

► **You can get several young plants from one leaf of *Begonia rex*.**

▲ **Raise these colourful coleus hybrids by sowing the seeds in late winter/early summer.**

◄ **Cut back *Euphorbia pulcherrima* (poinsettia) in early spring and use the new young shoots as cuttings.**

Plectranthus
Tip cuttings at 16°C (60°F) in spring.
Plumbago
Sow seeds or take cuttings at 16°C (60°F) in spring.
Primula
Surface sow seeds at 16°C (60°F) in summer.
Radermachera
Sow seeds at 21°C (70°F) in spring. Stem cuttings at 18°C (65°F) in summer.
Rhoeo
Sow seeds at 21°C (70°F) in spring. Take basal cuttings at 16°C (60°F) in mid-spring.
Rhoicissus
Take cuttings at 18°C (65°F) in spring.
Saintpaulia
Surface sow seeds at 21°C (70°F) in spring. Take leaf cuttings or divide at 21°C (70°F) in spring.
Sansevieria
Leaf cuttings or suckers at 21°C (70°F) in spring/summer.
Schefflera
Sow seeds at 21°C (70°F) in late winter.
Schizanthus
Sow seeds at 16°C (60°F) in spring/summer/early autumn.
Scindapsus
Tip, basal or leaf bud cuttings at 21°C (70°F) in spring.
Selaginella
Take cuttings at 16°C (60°F) in spring.
Solanum
Sow seeds at 18°C (65°F) in early spring. Tip cuttings at 16°C (60°F) in summer.
Spathiphyllum
Divide at 16°C (60°F) in mid-spring.
Stephanotis
Sow seeds at 21°C (70°F) in spring. Tip cuttings at 18°C (65°F) in early summer.

▲ Increase your stock of saintpaulias by sowing seeds, taking leaf cuttings or dividing mature plants.

Strelitzia
Sow seeds at 21°C (70°F) in early spring. Divide after flowering at 16°C (60°F).
Streptocarpus
Sow seeds at 18°C (65°F) in late winter. Leaf cuttings at 18°C (65°F) in summer.
Succulents
Surface sow seeds at 18°C (65°F) in spring. Remove offsets or take leaf cuttings at 18°C (65°F) in late spring/early summer.
Tolmiea
Root plantlets at 13°C (55°F) in spring/summer.
Torenia
Sow seeds at 18°C (65°F) in early spring.
Tradescantia
Tip cuttings at 16°C (60°F) in spring/summer.
Yucca
Root suckers at 16°C (60°F) in spring.
Zebrina
Tip cuttings at 16°C (60°F) in spring/summer.

· 15 ·
Vegetables and Culinary Herbs

The most common types of garden vegetable and culinary herb have been assembled here, in an A–Z format, by the common name, for at-a-glance reference on the best methods of propagation. All of the techniques referred to in the lists that follow are explained fully in the earlier chapters.

VEGETABLES

Artichoke globe
Sow seeds at 18°C (65°F) in late winter. Suckers – remove and replant 1 m (3 ft) apart in spring.
Artichoke Jerusalem
Plant tubers 15 cm (6 in) deep, 30 cm (12 in) apart in late winter/early spring.
Asparagus
Sow seeds 2.5 cm (1 in) deep. Plant one-year-old crowns outdoors in mid-spring.
Aubergine
Sow seeds at 18–21°C (65–70°F) late winter/early spring.
Bean, broad
Sow seeds outdoors late winter/early spring or late autumn for cropping in spring.
Bean, dwarf French
Sow seeds outdoors in late spring, or in pots in greenhouse early spring, to plant out under cloches mid-spring.
Bean, runner/climbing French
Sow seeds singly in pots in mid-spring, plant out after frost. Need supporting.
Beetroot
Sow seeds under cloches in early spring or outdoors in late spring.
Broccoli, green/sprouting
Sow in seed bed outdoors or in cold frame. Green in mid-spring, sprouting in late spring.
Brussels sprouts
Sow seeds in cold frame early spring or in outdoor seed bed mid-spring.
Cabbage
Sow spring varieties in seed bed mid or late summer. Sow summer varieties in greenhouse late winter or in seed bed mid-spring. Sow winter varieties in seed bed mid or late spring.
Carrot
Sow seeds under cloches late winter or outdoors early spring to mid summer.
Cauliflower
Sow under glass late winter or in seed bed mid-spring. Sow winter or spring varieties in seed bed mid or late spring.
Celeriac
Sow in greenhouse at 16–18°C (60–65°F) mid-spring.
Celery self blanching/trench
Surface sow at 16–18°C (60–65°F) in late winter/early spring.
Chicory and radicchio
Sow *in situ* early summer.
Courgette, see **Marrow**
Cucumber
Sow at 18°C (65°F). Indoor varieties in early spring, outdoor varieties mid or late spring.
Endive
Sow *in situ* early varieties in early summer, winter varieties in late summer.
Fennel Florence
Sow outdoors mid-spring to late summer.
Garlic
Plant cloves outdoors in mid or late autumn or late winter.
Kale (Borecole)
Sow in seed bed mid or late spring.
Kohl rabi
Sow outdoors mid spring to mid summer.
Leek
Sow at 16°C (60°F) in greenhouse in mid-spring or in seed bed in late spring/early summer.

Lettuce
Sow summer varieties in heated greenhouse in late winter or outdoors in early spring to late summer. Sow hardy winter varieties outdoors late summer/early autumn. Sow greenhouse varieties early autumn to late winter.
Marrow/courgette
Sow at 18°C (65°F) in mid-spring.
Melon
Sow under glass at 18°C (65°F) in mid-spring.
Onion
Sow indoors at 16°C (60°F) in late winter or outdoors in early spring. Sow winter hardy varieties outdoors in late summer/early autumn.
Pak choi
Sow *in situ* late spring to midsummer.
Parsnip
Sow outdoors in spring when soil temperature reaches 7°C (45°F).
Pea
Sow outdoors mid spring to early summer or round seeded varieties mid-autumn or late winter.
Pepper sweet/chilli
Sow indoors at 18°C (65°F) late winter to early spring.
Potato
Plant tubers under cloches late winter or outdoors early to mid-spring.
Pumpkin
Sow at 18°C (65°F) in mid-spring.
Radish
Sow *in situ* under cloches late winter or outdoors from early spring to mid-autumn.
Rhubarb
Sow seed outdoors in early spring. Divide crowns in late winter.
Salsify and scorzonera
Sow *in situ* in mid-spring.
Seakale
Take root cuttings (thongs) early or mid-spring.
Spinach
Sow *in situ* under cloches early spring or outdoors in late spring to early summer.
Spinach beet
Sow *in situ* in spring and midsummer for winter crops.
Swede
Sow *in situ* late spring to early summer.
Sweetcorn
Sow in heated greenhouse mid-spring or outdoors in late spring.
Tomato
Sow at 18°C (65°F) in late winter or early spring, outdoor varieties in early spring.
Turnip
Sow *in situ* from early spring to midsummer.

HERBS

Basil bush/sweet
Sow indoors in early spring.
Borage
Sow outdoors in mid-spring.
Chervil
Sow outdoors in early or mid-spring.
Chives
Sow seeds outdoors in early spring. Divide plants in spring or autumn.
Coriander
Sow outdoors in late spring.
Dill
Sow outdoors in mid-spring to midsummer.
Fennel
Sow outdoors in mid-spring to late summer. Divide in autumn.
Hyssop
Sow outdoors in mid or late spring. Divide in spring. Stem cuttings spring to autumn.
Lavender
Sow in cold frame or greenhouse in mid spring to early summer. Stem cuttings in spring or autumn.
Marjoram
Sow outdoors in mid or late spring. Divide in spring or autumn. Root or stem cuttings in late spring/early autumn.
Mint
Sow outdoors in early to late spring. Divide in spring or autumn. Root or stem cuttings in spring or autumn.
Oregano
Sow outdoors in mid or late spring. Divide in spring or autumn. Root or stem cuttings in late spring.
Parsley
Sow at 16°C (60°F) under glass or outdoors in spring.
Rosemary
Sow seeds indoors at 18°C (65°F) late winter/early spring or outdoors in early summer. Heel cuttings in early summer.
Sage
Sow outdoors in mid- or late spring. Stem cuttings in early summer.
Savory
Sow outdoors in mid- or late spring. Divide in spring or autumn. Stem cuttings in summer.
Sorrel
Sow outdoors in mid-spring.
Thyme
Sow outdoors in mid- or late spring. Divide or layer in spring or autumn. Heel cuttings in late spring/early summer.

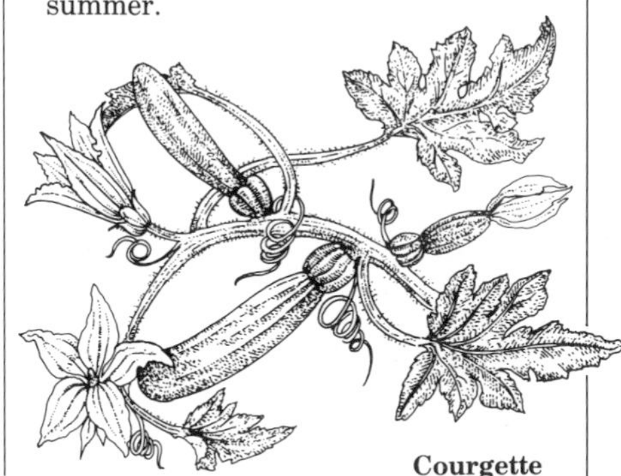
Courgette

· 16 ·
Hardy Fruit

The most common garden fruits have been listed in alphabetical order for at-a-glance reference on the best methods of propagation. Some of the techniques referred to in the lists that follow are explained fully in the earlier chapters. However, quite a number of fruits are propagated by grafting or budding. Normally, these are carried out by professional nurserymen as they are rather specialized and there are several ways of doing them.

Briefly, *grafting* is joining a stem, which is called a scion, of one plant onto the root, referred to as the stock, of another so that they grow as one tree. This restricts the eventual size of the fruit tree and encourages it to produce a crop earlier in life. Depending on which rootstock is used, a tree can be either 1.2–1.5 m (4–5 ft) high on an M27 rootstock to as tall as 5.4 m (18 ft) on an M111.

Budding is a form of grafting. A well-developed bud is taken from a healthy plant and inserted into a slit in the bark of another one with, in the case of fruit trees, a restricted root system. It has exactly the same result as grafting, but as a plant carries a lot more buds than stems, you can get more offspring from one parent at any one time.

Other trees and shrubs are grafted and budded for various reasons. For more detailed information, I suggest you refer to *The Complete Book of Propagation* by Graham Clarke and Alan Toogood, published by Ward Lock Ltd.

Apple
Budded in mid to late summer or grafted early to mid-spring onto restricting rootstocks. Sow seeds in autumn, but won't come true.

Apricot
Budded in mid to late summer or grafted in early spring onto St Julien A rootstock. Sow seeds in autumn, but won't come true.

Blackberry
Tip layer in spring or autumn.

◀ Apples are grafted or budded onto restricting woodstocks. If you raise them from seed they won't come true.

Blackcurrant
Hardwood cuttings 23 cm (9 in) long in autumn.

Blueberry/bilberry/blaeberry
Layer or take hardwood cuttings in autumn. Softwood cuttings in summer in a propagator.

Boysenberry
Tip layer in spring or autumn.

Cape gooseberry
Sow seeds singly at 16°C (60°F) in early spring.

Cherry
Budded in mid to late summer. Graft in early to mid-spring onto dwarfing Colt rootstock.

Cranberry
Divide in spring.

Damson
Budded in mid to late summer onto Pixy or St Julien A rootstock.

Dewberry
Tip layer in spring or autumn.

Fig
Heel cuttings 15 cm (6 in) long in a cold frame in summer. Layer in summer.

Gooseberry
Hardwood cuttings 25–30 cm (10–12 in) long in mid autumn. Strip off the lower buds leaving the top four or five. Layer in summer.

Grapes
Semi-hard bud cuttings in late winter/early spring. Hardwood cuttings 23 cm (9 in) long in mid/late autumn.
Hildaberry
Tip layer in spring or autumn.
Kiwi fruit
Semi-hard cuttings at 13°C (55°F) in mid/late summer. Sow seeds in spring or autumn in gentle heat, but they will not be true to type.
Loganberry
Tip layer in spring or autumn.
Marionberry
Tip layer in spring or autumn.
Medlar
Sow seeds in cold frame early/mid autumn. Named varieties do not come true from seed, they are grafted in mid spring or budded in summer.
Mulberry
Sow seeds under glass in early spring or out in the open in late spring. Cuttings 30 cm (12 in) long of ripened wood outdoors in spring or autumn.
Nectarine/peach
Graft or bud named varieties in mid summer onto St Julien A or seedling peach rootstock. Sow seeds in cold frame or cold greenhouse in autumn, but are not guaranteed to come true.
Pear
Grafted in spring or budded in summer onto Quince A or Quince C rootstocks. Sow seeds in autumn, but do not come true.
Plum
Budded onto Pixy or St Julien A rootstock in mid/late summer. Sow seed in autumn, but won't come true.
Quince
Hardwood cuttings 30 cm (12 in) long with a heel outdoors. Layer in early autumn.
Raspberry
Suckers in late autumn/early spring.
Redcurrant
Hardwood cuttings 25 cm (10 in) long outdoors in autumn. Remove all buds except the top 3 or 4. Layer in autumn.
Silvanberry
Tip layer in spring or autumn.
Strawberry
Runners in early-mid summer. Sow seeds in heated propagator in late winter/early spring.
Sunberry
Tip layer in spring or autumn.
Tayberry
Tip layer in spring or autumn.
Tummelberry
Tip layer in spring or autumn.
Veitchberry
Suckers in late autumn to early spring.
White currant As for redcurrant.
Wineberry
Tip layer in spring or autumn. Sow seeds in cold frame in autumn.
Worcesterberry
Hardwood cuttings 25–30 cm (10–12 in) long in mid autumn.
Youngberry
Tip layer in spring or autumn.

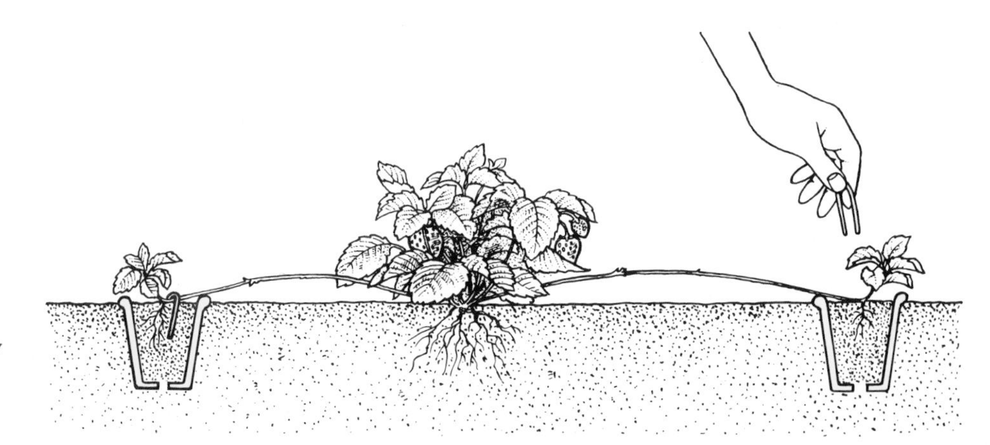

Fig. 23 Pegging strawberry runners down into pots of compost will make transplanting easier.

Index

Page numbers in *italics* indicate an illustration or boxed table.